TESTED BY *fire*

WILL WHAT YOU BUILD SURVIVE?

KELLEY LATTA

Carpenter's Son Publishing

Kelley
LATTA
MINISTRIES.llc

Tested by Fire: Will What You Build Survive?

© 2012, 2014 Kelley Latta
Revised Edition 2014

Published by Carpenter's Son Publishing, Franklin, Tennessee

Published in association with Larry Carpenter of Christian Book Services, LLC
www.christianbookservices.com

Cover Design by Frances Munoz/ www.BatresFreshDesign.com

Interior Design by Suzanne Lawing

Edited by Andrew Toy

ISBN: 978-1-940262-06-2

www.KelleyLattaMinistries.com

contents

about the author

KELLEY LATTA is a Bible teacher, event speaker, and author who digs deep into Scripture and brings it to life so that you can live transformed.

Having professed faith in Jesus as a child, Kelley was confronted in her mid-twenties by the realization that her beliefs about Christianity didn't match up with Jesus' teachings. Compelled into the Word to discover Truth for herself, she encountered Jesus through its pages and finally experienced the transforming power of grace. She now aims to help the body realize the saving reality of authentic intimacy with Jesus Christ.

Kelley serves at Hanover First Church of God in Hanover, Pennsylvania as a member of the Heart to Heart Women's Ministry team. She teaches a women's class on Sunday mornings and often leads a weekly Bible study, encouraging those around her to reach their fullest potential in Jesus.

Kelley also serves to strengthen and disciple the body of Christ online through Kelley Latta Ministries (www.KelleyLattaMinistries.com). Her weekly teaching blog, "Kelley's Word on Wednesday," will encourage you to live your faith and follow Jesus wholeheartedly. You can also find her sharing Truth on Facebook and Twitter.

Kelley is also the author of *Conversations with God: 40 days of Intimate Reflection*, a daily devotional that teaches how to meet God in His Word and respond to His voice.

Kelley joyfully shares her own faith adventure with her husband, Steve, and two teenage sons. When not writing or teaching, she can be found at the soccer fields watching her boys play or loving on their two Australian Shepherds. Her greatest hope is that her life will reflect the authentic character of Jesus.

introduction

Hello, beloved. I'm so glad you're considering taking this journey with me. I can tell you with confidence that transforming power and abundant life await you if you proceed with a humble heart. I speak from experience; my own excursion through these Scriptures dramatically changed me.

Born into a Christian home, I asked Jesus to be my Savior at a Christian school when I was a little girl. I attended church regularly and thought I understood what God wanted from me. Unfortunately, I never really bothered to ask Him. I made assumptions based on things I'd heard in church and set about living my life. And there lies the mistake that kept me from experiencing the fullness and abundance of life in Jesus Christ: I chose to live *my* life.

After 26 years of going through the motions of Christianity, I finally yielded to Jesus' tug at my heart and followed Him into His Word. There, as He spoke to me through the pages of divine text, I finally met my Savior and responded to Him with repentance. Grace began to change my thoughts and attitudes, and I realized that most of what I'd believed about Jesus had been wrong.

I have spent the last fifteen years pursuing the Lord who saved me, asking Him to teach me His truths and grow my understanding of His Word. He has faithfully lifted the veil on my deceptions bit by bit, and He has lovingly accompanied the light shed on my darkness with the power to overcome it.

Gratitude overwhelms me when I think of all He has done for me. As I contemplate the difference His grace has made in my life since I gave my life to follow Him, my heart aches for His body. I can't help but wonder how many "Christians" sit in the pews of our churches on Sunday mornings and remain as lost as I was. And many who *have* found Him remain isolated from the blessing of His love and bound in chains because they don't understand the Scriptures. God Himself said in Hosea 4:6, "*my people are destroyed from lack of knowledge.*"

If that's you, dear one, I offer you hope. His name is Jesus—the real Jesus— Faithful and True. May you encounter the King of Kings and experience God's salvation as He intended, and may your life begin to flourish with the abundant fruit of grace.

Kelley

BUILDING ON A FIRM FOUNDATION

God's solid foundation stands firm, sealed with this inscription:
"The Lord knows those who are his," and,
"Everyone who confesses the name of the Lord
must turn away from wickedness."

2 TIMOTHY 2:19

day 1 : FOUNDED ON THE ROCK

Welcome, friend. A journey brimming with discovery awaits us. I pray that as we venture together in search of the treasures appointed for us in God's Word, we will encounter the most precious treasure of all: Christ Himself. As He reveals Himself in a new and glorious way, may our own hearts echo the cry of the Apostle Paul,

> *. . . I consider everything a loss compared to the surpassing greatness of knowing Christ Jesus my Lord . . .*
> (PHILIPPIANS 3:8)

For most of my life, I did not know Jesus. I knew the facts, but I didn't know the Man. If you asked me, I would have told you I knew Him. I could've even given you Scripture to back it up. Salvation by grace, as I understood it, seemed a pretty simple thing. Yet a nagging uncertainty robbed me of the peace Scripture promised I would have in Jesus. And once I finally answered the prompting to check God's Word to find out why, I discovered that I had, indeed, been standing on very shaky ground.

God has invited you here to consider whether the foundation on which you currently build your life consists of solid rock or shifting sand. Why the need? As Jesus taught in the seventh chapter of Matthew, a house that isn't founded on the rock is doomed. As the rain pours down, the streams rise, and the winds beat against it, it will fall *"with a great crash"* (Matthew 7:27).

Before time ever was, God planned to build a house. He began its construction with the nation of Israel, His chosen possession through whom He would reveal His glory to the world. *"But now in Christ Jesus you who once were far away have been brought near through the blood of Christ"* (Ephesians 2:13). We have been invited through Christ to become members of

Do you know the One you claim to have believed?

His royal house!

God ordained very particular plans for His house. A stone would support the structure, providing its strength and ensuring the lasting nature of its construction.

- List every descriptive detail given about this stone in **Isaiah 28:16**.

  a stone for a sure foundation -
  a tried stone -

  _____

- According to this verse, who will never be dismayed?

  _____

Ephesians 2:19-22 provides more information about the dwelling God is building. Please read the passage, asking God to reveal its meaning.

- According to **verse 19**, what have we become in Christ?

  _____

  _____

- On what are we, as God's household, built (**verse 20**)?

  _____

  - Who is the chief cornerstone? _____

- What is Christ's role in the building process (**verse 21**)?

  _____

  _____

- What is your role in the building process (**verse 22**)?

  _____

Jesus Christ is the Cornerstone, the tested and sure foundation through whom God will bring about all His plans and build the house He has designed. You'll notice that even your role, "*to* become a dwelling in which God lives by His Spirit," can only be accomplished "in Him."

If we want to be certain of our membership in God's house and partake of the blessing of eternal life that accompanies it, Jesus must be our Rock. He must be the sure foundation supporting all we do. How can we be certain we're securely held for eternity within the safety of the Rock? Isaiah 28:16 has already revealed our answer,

> The one who **trusts** will never be dismayed
> (emphasis mine).

To secure our passage into the house of God, we must trust Jesus with our very lives. John 3:16 states clearly, *"For God so loved the world that he gave his one and only Son, that whoever believes in him shall not perish but have eternal life."*

We cannot earn our way into God's house. We must simply receive the lavish gift of grace poured out to us through His Son. Our receipt of this gift occurs the moment we *believe* in Him.

To ensure we understand exactly what it means to believe in Jesus, God provided specific instructions for us through the pen of the Apostle Paul. Please read **Romans 10:8-11**.

- **Verse 9** offers two clear commands necessary for salvation. What are they?

    1. _____

    2. _____

Verse 11 references Isaiah 28:16 and sums up the teaching, suggesting, "Anyone who trusts *according to these two commands* will never be put to shame."

Scripture teaches that to receive the gift of salvation offered by God through His Son, we must believe that Jesus is God made flesh who died for our sin and rose again. We must also confess Him as Lord. At first glance, confessing "Jesus is Lord" may seem a simple thing, but Jesus offers a warning in **Matthew**

Jesus said: "Not everyone who says to me, 'Lord, Lord,' will enter the kingdom of heaven, but only he who does the will of my Father who is in heaven."
—MATTHEW 7:21

7:21-23 that we would be wise to heed. Please read the passage, asking God to open your heart to the truth of His Word.

- What does **verse 21** teach about the people who call Jesus "Lord"?

_____

  - Who exactly *will* enter the kingdom?

  _____

- According to **verse 22**, why will many who call Jesus "Lord" claim they deserve access to heaven?

_____

_____

  - In whose "name" did they claim to do these works?

  _____

- According to Jesus' own words, what will be His response to these people when He returns?

_____

_____

Oh, that none of us would hear those condemning words of Christ on the Day of Judgment, *"I never knew you. Away from me you evil doers!"*

Precious one, I draw your attention to this passage of Scripture, not to instill fear, but to reveal truth so that you can make a discerning judgment as to whether you stand on the right side of it. These *many* that Jesus foretold about in Matthew 7 believed they were His. They called Him Lord with their mouths. They produced works in His name as evidence of their belief. *Yet they did not belong to Him.* They will pay for that shortcoming for all eternity.

What had they missed? If we want to be certain we won't be listed among those cast aside at Christ's return, we must discern the root of their misconception. Fortunately, Jesus' warning also includes His answer in verse 21: calling Jesus "Lord" with our mouths doesn't cut it if we aren't willing to take up the will of the Father.

Let's revisit Scripture's command in Romans 10:9 to *"confess with your mouth, 'Jesus is Lord.'"* Obviously, there's more to this Scripture than meets the eye. Perhaps a look at the meaning of the words will open our understanding.

The Greek word Jesus used that we translate "confess" is *homologeō*, which means to promise or agree. It suggests making a declaration of intent. According to the *Theological Dictionary of the New Testament*, the aim of its meaning is "not a theoretical agreement which does not commit us, but acceptance of a common cause."[1]

Even more important to our understanding is the meaning of the word "Lord." The Greek word *kýrios* means *lord* or *master*, and is defined as "one who possesses and exercises power and authority and to whom respect is thus ascribed." It's used to indicate a superior rank, and can also encompass the meanings of *owner and husband.* [2]

In basic terms, to confess that Jesus is Lord is to declare your intent to make Him Lord and Master over your life, taking up His cause in place of your own. In other words, in order to rest in the secure grip of the Rock, you must relinquish the ownership rights to your life and hand them to Jesus.

God freely offers salvation to all through the gift of His Son, but this gift of life is not without cost (Luke 14:27-28). To receive His gift of grace and pass through the doorway to eternal life, you must make an exchange. You must voluntarily choose to lay down your will—your choices, preferences and desires—and take up the will of the Father.

Throughout the ages, God has invited humanity to live according to His plan in the safety of His protection. Repeatedly,

Confess "Jesus is Lord": Declare Him Lord and Master over your life. Agree to let Jesus lead.

---

1. *Vol. 5: Theological Dictionary of the New Testament.* 1964- (G. Kittel, G. W. Bromiley & G. Friedrich, Ed.) (electronic ed.) (200). Grand Rapids, MI: Eerdmans.

2. Myers, A. C. (1987). *The Eerdmans Bible Dictionary* (661). Grand Rapids, Mich.: Eerdmans.

man has chosen to govern himself and go his own way rather than trust the God who created him. In Christ, God now offers the power to overcome the deceptive allure of our own nature and escape our sin and its consequence so that we may return to Him. But we must reject our old nature and point our compass steadfastly in the direction of His will for us instead of our own. That, my friend, conveys a heart of repentance, *"Repent and believe the good news!"* (Mark 1:15).

Your Creator beckons you to eternal glory.

> *"For I know the plans I have for you,"* declares the Lord, *"plans to prosper you and not to harm you, plans to give you hope and a future"* (JEREMIAH 29:11).

God's plan for you is a good plan. He means to enrich your life and cause it to flourish with the fruit of His kingdom. If you will trust Him to write your story, He offers the promise of a glorious, eternal future.

One question looms between you and the fulfillment of all God's promises. Will you believe?

day 2: He Who Has Ears, Let Him Hear

Welcome back, dear one. Your time spent seeking God through His Word will not be wasted. He will multiply your offering to Him and return it to you as a fruitful harvest. May we learn to partake fully in the blessings and riches of our faith in Jesus!

Yesterday we laid the first stone, setting the sure foundation for membership into God's house: *Jesus.* He is the Cornerstone (Eph 2:20), the Word made flesh (John 1:14), the bright Morning Star (Rev 22:16), and the Gate (John 10:9) to all of God's promises. Only in and through Him can we gain eternal life in heaven and abundant life on earth. Let's begin our time together today celebrating the Light of life (John 8:12). Please read **Colossians 1:15-20**.

> *Today's Truth:*
>
> "Give ear and come to me; hear me, that your soul may live."
> —Isaiah 55:3

- What two details does **verse 15** give about Jesus?

   1. _____

   2. _____

- According to **verse 16**, who created *all* things?

   _____

   - Why were they created?

      _____

- Please write **verse 17** on the lines below.

   _____

   _____

- What is Christ's role in the church (**verse 18**)?

   _____

- What was God pleased to do in **verse 19**?

   _____

• What did God do through Christ (**verse 20**)?

_____

_____

Jesus Christ is the source of all things, and He alone is the One for whom they exist. *"I am the Alpha and the Omega, the First and the Last, the Beginning and the End"* (Revelation 22:13). He always was, He always will be, and *"in him all things hold together"* (verse 17). For anything to have lasting quality, Jesus must dwell at the center of it.

Notice the significance of verse 18. Christ's role in the church is to reign supreme as the Head of the body.

For anything to have lasting quality, Jesus must dwell at its center.

Consider the workings of our physical bodies. The head governs the actions of each body part. A foot cannot take a step without receiving a message from the brain to move. Fingers cannot do their work without receiving a directive to do so from the central nervous system. So it is with Christ's body. The body snaps into action in response to commands communicated from the Head—Jesus— through our central nervous system: the Holy Spirit.

With that in mind, let's explore Jesus' parable of the wise and foolish builders. Please read **Matthew 7:24-27**, asking God for fresh insight.

• According to Christ, what will distinguish between one who builds upon the rock and one who builds on sinking sand?

_____

We have already established that Jesus Himself is the Rock, the Chief Cornerstone and sure foundation through whom we are saved. We become His as we believe in the cleansing power of His sacrifice for our sin and make a commitment to follow Him.

Our salvation does not signal the end of our journey but the beginning. Once we're saved, God watches to see what we will do with what we've been given. As long as we live on this earth, we continue to build something—either a monument to the glory of the Lord or a testament to our love for ourselves.

Jesus' illustration teaches that only dwellings built on the firm foundation of rock will stand against the coming storms. Everything we build on enticingly beautiful sandy shores will be washed away in an instant by the raging tides. As believers, we need to know how to distinguish between the two.

In theory, that may seem an obvious distinction. In reality, it's not so clear. Our adversary, the deceiver, seeks to sabotage the building process, and he is remarkably gifted at camouflaging shifting sand to give it the appearance of solid rock.

• What does **2 Corinthians 11:14** reveal about our enemy?

_____

Verse 15 adds the uncomfortable truth that the devil's servants also masquerade as servants of righteousness. We face the biblical reality that not all those who claim to be followers of Christ truly are. Many people within our churches bear the appearance of Christianity, but inwardly their hearts bend toward obedience to another; they remain bound to their own sin nature instead of Jesus Christ. This means we must be extremely diligent to know God's Word for ourselves, so we cannot be deceived and led astray from God and His purpose (2 Cor. 11:3).

According to our passage in Matthew 7, two things will determine whether we build on a sure foundation of rock:

1. Do we hear what God speaks to us through His Son?
2. Are we committed to doing what He says?

We will spend the rest of today celebrating the first truth Christ illuminates in this parable: God speaks. I pray that this truth is already a vivid reality in your life, but I will confess to you that for a long time, it never occurred to me to consider that God might speak to me. I knew that He *could* speak—He spoke creation into existence—and I knew that He *used to* speak through the prophets to lead His people. But the thought that He *still speaks* to us today and wants to speak to me never even entered my mind. If you can relate and the idea that God speaks to you seems a little surprising and unfamiliar, rejoice that you are about to experience a new revelation of God in your life.

Please read **Hebrews 1:1-3.**

- According to **verse 2**, how has God spoken to us "*in these last days?*"

  _____

  - What other two pieces of information are we given about Jesus in this verse?

    1. _____

    2. _____

God speaks today through His Son.

- How does **verse 3** describe Jesus' relationship to the Father?

  _____

  _____

  - By what does Jesus "*sustain all things?*"

    _____

And, "*After He had provided purification for sins, He sat down at the right hand of the Majesty in heaven*" (verse 3). These verses reveal Jesus to be the Creator of the world, the Heir and Sustainer of all things, the Radiance of God's glory, the One who purifies us from sin, and the Way in which God has chosen to communicate to His people in these days. Jesus is *everything* to us, and *all things* are sustained by His powerful Word. If we want to remain on the foundation that cannot be shaken, we must build using only the words of the Chief Cornerstone.

Just as He did in the days of the prophets, God still communicates His will to His people. He has given us Jesus, the Head of the body, to direct and lead us. The question is: Do we *hear* Him? Are we even tuning in?

Whether or not we hear God is of great significance in Scripture. In Isaiah 55:3 God petitions us, "*Give ear and come to me; hear me, that your soul may live.*" Notice that our soul's capacity to *live* will be determined by whether or not we come near to God to hear Him. Consider this truth: we will only draw near to hear if we are inclined to know and live God's will.

> *The ability to hear God is one of the marks of the Holy Spirit that reveals itself in a true believer.*

- Please write **John 8:47** on the lines below.

_____

_____

_____

Do you know who you belong to? Jesus died to redeem you from the power of sin so you could be reconciled to a Holy God. He bore the beatings, the lashes, the thorns and the nails to tear the curtain keeping you from His presence. Have you accepted His invitation and passed through the opening?

Every believer possesses the ability to hear from God.

If you're not certain, take heart. *"Now is the time of God's favor, now is the day of salvation"* (2 Corinthians 6:2). To the heart that desires to know Him, He will make Himself known. Approach the throne of grace, confess your sin, and ask for the gift of His presence. Invite Jesus to lead you to a new life in Him. As He opens your ears to hear Him, respond in faith that your soul may live.

day 3: DISCERNING THE STILL, SMALL VOICE

Yesterday we celebrated the unfathomable truth that the God of the universe chooses to speak to man because He desires sweet fellowship with His creation. He gave us His Son as a sacrifice for our sin so that we could return to Him and become His possession. If you have entered into relationship with Jesus Christ by receiving Him into your heart to rule and reign as Lord and Savior, you already have the ability to hear Him speak to you. Now you must discover how to discern what He is saying.

Calling Himself the Good Shepherd, Jesus paints a vivid portrait of the life of the believer in **John 10**. Please read **verses 1-18**, asking God to open your mind to the truth of His Word.

• What specific action will Christ's "sheep" take in **verse 3**?

_____

• What does Christ do for His sheep?

_____

_____

• According to **verse 4,** as Jesus goes on ahead of His sheep, what will they do?

_____

• Why?

_____

Verse 5 brings sadness to my heart. For far too many of us, Jesus is the stranger. We are so used to tuning our ears to the shouts of the world that we cannot recognize the tender whisper of the Shepherd beckoning us to safe pasture. If we do hear Him, often His voice is so unfamiliar and contrary to what we're used to hearing that we tend to run the other way. Unfortunately, running away from Christ leads us straight into the clutches of the enemy of our souls.

- According to **verse 10**, what is the goal of our enemy, the thief?

  _____

  - What is the goal of the Shepherd?

  _____

Dear one, this verse reveals why salvation must come to us by faith alone. The one in whom we place our faith—the lord we choose to exalt as our master and trust with the role of governing our lives—determines our ultimate destination. Will we trust and allow the thief, the prince of this world (John 12:31), to continue governing our steps as he has since the fall? Or will we offer control of our lives to Jesus Christ and commit ourselves to following the voice of the Shepherd? We can't have it both ways. We place our faith in either one or the other.

Many try to tap into the abundance of Christ without recognizing the need to know Him intimately. We will never know His abundance without first knowing Him. We must learn to embrace and trust the One who *"lays down His life for the sheep"* (verse 11).

We will never know Christ's abundance without first knowing Him.

- According to **verses 14-15**, how intimately do we have the capacity to know Christ?

  _____

- How well does Christ know the Father (**verse 30**)?

  _____

Precious one, as the redeemed, we are meant to be *one* with Christ—one in Spirit, one in our hearts, one in our minds, and one with our lives. He is our Head, and we the members of His body, moving in accordance with His will to fulfill His purpose.

- Please write **Philippians 2:13** on the lines below.

  _____

  _____

God intends for each of us to align our will and our actions with His perfect purpose. God Himself does the work; our role is to yield in cooperation. We will break down this process over the next few weeks in biblical detail, but today we will focus on discovering how to draw near to hear the voice of the Shepherd.

The primary way Jesus speaks to us is through His Word.

- According to **2 Timothy 3:16,** where does Scripture come from?

_____

- What is it useful for?

_____

_____

Scripture comes to us straight from the mouth of God. The words etched on the pages of our Bibles are not derived from the thoughts of man. The Spirit of Christ Himself moved the pens of the authors, and its power remains as real and relevant today as it was when Jesus walked the dusty roads of Galilee. However, we often miss its power because of our approach to it.

We can diligently study Scripture and miss experiencing its life.

- What warning does Jesus give in **John 5:39-40?**

_____

_____

Did you know that you can be a *diligent* student of the Word and yet miss its life? Christ reveals the missing element in these verses. We must learn to *come to Him* through its pages.

So often we approach the Word of God as a textbook. As 2 Timothy 3:16 directs us, we use it for teaching, training, and correcting—and we should! But in doing so, we often ignore its primary purpose: the communication of Jesus to the members of His body. The text can give guidelines to the corporate body, but only the Spirit of Christ communicating through the text can speak life to an individual.

- Jesus spoke a revelation to a thirsty woman at a well in **John 4:23-24.** According to these verses, how must one worship to be a *true* worshiper?

_____

Prior to Christ's death on a cross, followers generally approached Scripture as a book of law—God's instructions to His people that they must obey to receive His blessing. We often act as if that hasn't changed! But Christ's sacrifice for us opened up something marvelous: the ability to hear, interact with, and be changed by an unseen God.

Please read **John 16:7-15.**

- Why did Jesus tell His disciples that it was for their good He was going away (**verse 7**)?

_____

- What does **verse 8** indicate is one of the roles of the Counselor?

_____

- **Verse 13** teaches that the Spirit of Truth will *"guide you into all truth."* What will He speak?

_____

- How will He bring glory to Christ (**verse 14**)?

_____

_____

The role of the Counselor, the Spirit of Truth, is imperative to the prosperity and completion of God's promises in the life of a believer. Salvation can only take place as we acknowledge and answer Him (John 6:44), and any further work of God in our lives will only occur as we interact with and continue to respond to Him.

John 16 reveals some of the roles God intends for His Spirit to assume in our lives.

- He will convict us of our guilt in regard to sin and righteousness.
- He will guide us in truth, speaking only what He hears from the Word of truth, Jesus.
- Verse 13 even reveals the glorious promise that the Spirit of Christ will tell us what is yet to come!

The Spirit is God's gift to us, given to guide us along the path of His will. He is our personal Counselor, who takes what He hears from Jesus and makes it known to us. And He will do it as we assume the posture of a true worshiper; we must unite the Spirit with the Truth.

Fellowship with the Holy Spirit is imperative to your prosperity as a believer.

Every time you open the Word of God, invite His Spirit to meet you and lead you through its pages. Only His Spirit can bring to life words written in a centuries-old text, making them powerful, alive and active (Hebrews 4:12). Expect Christ Himself to meet you through His Word, and then glory in wonder as the Book of Law transforms itself into the Book of Life. Seek *Him* through His Word, and you will experience the fulfillment of His promise,

Your word is a lamp to my feet and a light for my path
(Psalm 119:105).

The only thing left to do then is follow.

day 4: THE WAR OF THE WILL

I pray that even now, as you work your way through this study, you are beginning to hear God speak to you through His Son. Most often His voice isn't accompanied by trumpet blasts and thunder claps. It's whispered into your heart by the Spirit within you, and you must incline your ear to hear His message. Yet when you do hear those Words of life rising up to you through the pages of Scripture, their power and effect in your life will be decided by your response to what you hear.

Please read **James 1:22-25.**

• What command are we given in **verse 22**?

_____

    • If we don't do what we hear, what are we doing?

_____

• According to **verse 25**, what result follows our obedience?

_____

We deceive ourselves when we hear God's Word and choose to ignore it. You see, God's power is released into our lives by faith. Responding to what we've heard with obedience demonstrates trust, and *"the one who trusts will never be dismayed"* (Isaiah 28:16).

Let's recall our two points drawn earlier this week from Matthew 7:24-27, Jesus' parable of the wise and foolish builder. If we are going to build on the solid foundation of rock, these two things must be true of us:

1. We must seek to hear Jesus speaking to us through His Word.
2. When we hear, we must do what He says.

Do you ever have a problem with follow through? We can have the very best intentions to do what's been asked of us, but when it gets right down to it, it just doesn't happen. This seems to be the mantra for my sons' adolescent years.

Simple instructions like, "Please put your dirty socks in your hamper or in the laundry room," are answered eagerly with, "Okay, Mom." Yet somehow as they attempt to follow through, the promise is forgotten, and the action translates to: whip off my socks when my feet get hot and leave them wherever I happen to be.

We often offer the same type of response to God's instructions to us. With hearts full of worship on Sunday morning, we lift our hands and say, "Yes, Lord!" But when the time comes to actually trust and follow, our actions don't translate into obedience. Jesus gives a biblical answer to this dilemma in **Matthew 26:41**.

> *We must live with an acute awareness of our own capacity to fall.*

• Why do we often fail with the follow through?

_____

_____

• What does Jesus recommend we do so we don't fall into temptation to disobey?

_____

We must live with an acute awareness of our own capacity to fall. 1 Corinthians 10:12 offers this word of warning, *"So, if you think you are standing firm, be careful that you don't fall!"* Our spirits may be willing, but we ourselves, in our sin-ravaged, fallen bodies are extremely weak. Praise God, we have a source of strength in our weakness!

Please read **2 Corinthians 12:9**, asking God to open your understanding of His Word.

• Hear Jesus speaking to you, *"My Grace is sufficient for you."* What does that promise mean to you?

_____

_____

- What is made perfect in our weakness?

_____

- According to Paul, when would Christ's power rest on him?

_____

_____

When we humble ourselves to openly acknowledge and admit our weakness, we open the door for the power of Christ to rest on us. His glorious strength is made perfect in our lives as He fills the gap, and our weakness is overcome by His strength. That's why Jesus calls us to pray in Matthew 26:41. In our own power, we will succumb to temptation and fall, but in Him, we have the capacity to overcome.

- Please write **Romans 8:37** on the lines below.

_____

_____

_____

Praise God for Him who loved us, Amen?

Let's consider our struggle to obey. **Galatians 5:16-18** offers us insight into the cause of our struggle. Please read the passage, asking God to give you understanding of its meaning.

- Explain the conflict described in **verse 17**.

_____

_____

- According to this verse, what will be the inevitable result of allowing this conflict to remain?

_____

- According to **verse 16**, how can we keep from giving in to the desires of our sinful nature?

_____

Living by the Spirit is further defined for us in verse 18, *"But if you are **led by the Spirit**, you are not under law"* (emphasis mine).

From the moment we put our faith in Jesus and His Spirit makes His home within us, our own fallen nature begins to rise up in conflict with His leadership, trying to hold onto its former position of authority. Each time the Spirit begins to move us in the direction of His will, our sinful nature will work diligently to lead us steadfastly in the opposite direction. When we allow ourselves to waver between allegiance to our own nature and obedience to Christ, we abide in conflict. The result of allowing such conflict to remain is revealed in verse 17, *"you do not do what you want."*

Wavering between following your flesh and the Spirit will always result in sin.

If we do not purposefully commit each day to reject the leadership of our own nature and submit instead to following the leadership of Christ's Spirit, we will end up giving in to sin and doing what we don't want to do—*every* time.

Why? Because Jesus insists that we *choose* Him. Unlike our enemy who desires to keep us as slaves, Jesus requests our love. And love, my friend, is offered. He will not simply take His authority over us. He waits for us to give it to Him.

Our disobedience quenches the power of the Spirit within us and strengthens the power of our flesh. But when we choose to offer our love to Jesus by sincerely pursuing obedience to His leadership, we begin to tap into His power to overcome. 1 John 4:4 delivers this wonderful promise:

> *You, dear children, are from God and have overcome them, because the one who is in you is greater than the one who is in the world.*

When we set our hearts on choosing obedience to Jesus Christ, His Spirit within us empowers us to overcome our sinful nature and fulfill God's will. As we become vessels who not only *hear* His Word to us but also *do* as He says, we begin to build on His sure foundation. Consequently, we will be wrapped in the safety of His protection and equipped to stand against the coming storms (Matthew 7:24-27).

Build only on the sure foundation of obedience to God's will spoken to you through Christ, and you will experience the promise of James 1:25:

> . . . *[s]he will be blessed in what [s]he does.*

Are you ready to follow Jesus to your blessing?

day 5: A LIVING SACRIFICE

God is at work all around us, drawing lost souls to Himself as He builds and strengthens His church. Do you *see* Him?

Dear one, God isn't hiding; many of us simply aren't *seeking*. We've wandered from Him, stumbling down a path forged by our own desires and have expected God to meet us there. We've been deceived. The key to finding ourselves amidst a glorious display of God's grace and power as we watch Him work the miraculous is to position ourselves smack dab in the middle of His will.

History repeatedly teaches that God's people experienced an outpouring of His favor and a display of His might as they chose to trust God through obedience instead of operating according to their own plans and goals. Nothing has changed. If we wish to see God reveal Himself, we must surrender our own ideas and plans and submit ourselves completely by faith to His.

That leaves us seeking the answer to this vital question. How can we discern what God's will is?

The answer often eludes the majority of Christ's followers. Most struggle with an inability to know His will and are often left guessing. When we're not sure what to do, we tend to go with what we know, making our decisions based on our own understanding. Then we wonder why God hasn't shown up.

- **Proverbs 14:12** holds such significance for us, God chose to repeat it again in **Proverbs 16:25**. Please write the verse on the lines below.

  _____

  _____

Too often we rely on what *seems* right to us. We make decisions based on our feelings and our logic, and we justify it with the argument that God gave us our brains so we'd use them. We embrace the reasoning of the world and find comfort in its encouragement to "follow your heart."

Allow me to give you a word of warning from the mouth of God. *"The heart is deceitful above all things and beyond cure"* (Jeremiah 17:9).

On their own, our hearts and minds cannot be trusted. The powerful allure of our sinful nature will lead us straight down a path to our destruction. We must learn to filter our feelings and thoughts through the authority and leadership of Jesus Christ.

- What does **Proverbs 3:5-6** tell us about relying on our own understanding?

_____

_____

Scripture repeatedly claims that God will reveal the path to us. He's not hiding His will. Our problem comes in discerning it.

We've already discussed the need to allow Jesus to speak to us through His Word. Now we will consider the posture and attitude we must adopt to be able to discern His will. Read **Romans 12:1-2.**

- According to **verse 1**, what does God say is our spiritual act of worship?

_____

- **Verse 2** lists two commands, the first indicating what we should *not* do, the second teaching what we should do instead. What are they?

  1. _____

  2. _____

- What will happen as a result of following these two commands?

_____

_____

There you have it, the answer to the ever-elusive question of how to discover God's will. He asks two things of us. The first is that we don't try to conform to the world's standards. If our goal is to blend in with everybody else, we can expect God to keep His distance. He's in the business of revealing Himself through the extraordinary. If we try to follow the patterns of the world, embracing what seems to work for everyone else, we'll miss our opportunity to see God.

The second thing He commands is to be transformed by the renewing of our minds. Why is this so important? Recall yesterday's study of Galatians 5:16-18. A battle of wills rages within you. Your sinful nature and the Spirit are at war, and each seeks your allegiance. You will submit your obedience to the will of the one you allow to govern your thoughts.

It's time to go to battle and reclaim control of your mind. Read **2 Corinthians 10:3-5.**

You will live out the will of whatever influence you allow to govern your thoughts.

• As believers, what power do the weapons given to us have (**verse 4**)?

_____

• According to **verse 5**, what is a stronghold?

_____

_____

• And how do we demolish them?

"*. . . we take _____ every _____ to make it _____ to Christ.*"

How do we become transformed by the renewing of our minds as God commands in Romans 12:2? We ask the Spirit of Christ to shed His light on any thought we possess that doesn't line up with His perfect Word. As He complies and alerts us to a thought pattern that leads us astray, we then have the responsibility to take it captive, refusing to allow it power over us any longer. Next, we must replace the worldly thought with God's Truth as He reveals it to us in His Word.

We cannot expect to hear God communicating His will to us without actively cooperating with Christ to alter our thinking. If we choose to remain bound to our old patterns of thought, we choose to conform to the world and reject Jesus in the process.

Verse 1 teaches that we must present ourselves to the Lord as a living sacrifice. He asks that we give ourselves fully to Him— heart, soul, mind, and body— surrendering our lives to Jesus as an offering that may be used of Him for His glory. Only then, according to verse 2, will we *"be able to test and approve what God's will is—His good, pleasing and perfect will."*

Romans 12 is not the only place we find this principle revealed in Scripture. Ask God to penetrate your heart with His truth, and please read **Luke 9:23-26**.

- According to Jesus, what three things must one do to be His true disciple (**verse 23**)?

  1. _____

  2. _____

  3. _____

- What does Jesus challenge us to do instead of saving or preserving our life as we know it (**verse 24**)?

  _____

- What does Jesus suggest will happen to a man who "gains the whole world," obviously allowing the world's standards to govern his thoughts and actions (**verse 25**)?

  _____

- What specifically will cause Jesus to be ashamed of us when He returns in glory (**verse 26**)?

  _____

Once again we discover the now familiar mention of Jesus' words gracing the pages of Scripture. This time Jesus declares that anyone ashamed of His words will bring shame upon himself at His return.

We must embrace Christ's words to us with hearts set on obedience. In verse 23, Jesus describes the role of a true disciple, one whose feet are set firmly on the Rock. You'll notice based on the wording of the verse that these commands are not optional.

First, He challenges us to deny ourselves. I imagine your initial reaction to that command was not positive. Why would it be? The self that Jesus asks you to deny is your sinful nature, and as we've discussed, it will not willingly relinquish its control over you. What's more, it tells you that you don't really want it to.

But, ultimately, you must decide what you believe. If you trust that Jesus truly is *for you*, that He is the *Way* and the *Truth* and the *Life*, then why not trust Him to lead? The only thing that would keep you from wanting to deny your self is that you don't really *believe* it's worth it.

Second, He commands us to take up our cross. An image of our bloodied Lord carrying His own cross to His execution floods my mind. Death lies at the end of the road tread under the weight of a cross. How could this be God's plan for you?

Death must always precede resurrection life.

- According to **John 11:25**, what happens to one who "dies" believing in Jesus?

_____

Dear one, death must always precede resurrection life! Jesus desires to pour His abundance into your life, but the powerful rule of sin forestalls His blessing. Sin must die in you for new life in Christ to be revealed. Do you believe the life Christ offers is worth whatever it may cost?

The cross Jesus asks you to take up represents God's perfect will for you. It sets you on the path to abundant life and includes the removal of sin along the way. Notice how often we're required to take up that cross. *Daily*. The war between our old nature and Christ's Spirit will not cease until His return. We must daily choose to take up God's will, or we will automatically default back to our old patterns and ways.

Once we have committed to deny our old self and take up the cross of God's will, there is but one thing left to do. *Follow*. And as we present ourselves to Him a living sacrifice, committing to keep in step with His Spirit, we will see God work the miraculous . . . first *within* us, and then *through* us.

I pray you allow Him to give you a front row seat to the revelation of His glory!

Reflections on Week 1

TO LIVE BY FAITH

*"But my righteous one will live by faith.
And if he shrinks back, I will not be pleased with him."
But we are not of those who shrink back and are destroyed,
but of those who believe and are saved.*

HEBREWS 10:38-39

day 1: GOD'S LOVE LANGUAGE

Welcome back, friend. Today we will begin with one of my favorite Scriptures. Ask God to speak to your heart, and please read **John 14:15-21.**

- According to **verse 15**, what will one who loves Jesus do?

_____

- **Verse 17** teaches that the world can't see or accept the Spirit of Truth, but—praise Jesus—believers can! Why?

_____

- Jesus had to leave after His crucifixion, but He promised the disciples He would not abandon them. What did He tell them in **verse 18**?

_____

- **Verse 19** delivers two wonderful promises to believers. What are they?

  1. _____

  2. _____

- **Verse 21** reemphasizes verse 15, *"Whoever has my commands and obeys them, he is the one who loves me."* What promise does Jesus make regarding those who love Him?

_____

_____

For 26 years, I wondered why I never saw Jesus at work in my life. I went to church and did my best to please Him. I could recite all the books in both the Old and New Testaments, and I had memorized dozens of Scriptures, earning the praises of my Sunday school teachers. Yet envy tugged at my heart when I had occasion to hear various believers share all that Jesus had done for them. You see, I didn't have a testimony.

Through all those years of attending church, I could identify no tangible evidence of grace in my life. Because of that, I often struggled over the question of whether Jesus was even real. Then one day, the Spirit lifted the veil on my deception and hit me right between the eyes with this truth. *I didn't love Him.* And God's Word is clear. Jesus shows Himself to those who do.

- In **Mark 12:28**, Jesus is asked, *"Of all the commandments, which is the most important?"* Write His answer from **verses 29-30** on the lines below.

_____

_____

_____

_____

Jesus taught that our highest priority above all else is to accept God as the one true God, and love Him with everything we've got. Not just with our heart, but with all our soul, our entire mind, and all our strength. Jesus essentially said, "If you take nothing else from Scripture, take this. Love God with everything you are."

Dear one, is Jesus actively revealing Himself in your life? Can you offer testimony of the ways Jesus has shown Himself to you personally? If your answer to those questions is no, John 14:21 likely discloses the reason. Jesus promises to reveal Himself to those who love Him.

Love can be a tricky thing, particularly since our hearts deceive us. I learned early on to say that I loved Jesus. I repeated it enough that I even convinced myself to believe it. After all, it was the *right* response; all good Christians love Jesus!

But according to God's Word, love for Jesus is more than a warm feeling in your heart as you worship. It requires the participation of the mind and involves a show of strength that includes the cooperation of the will. Love, according to God's vocabulary, is expressed by obedience to His commands.

- Please write **1 John 5:3-4** on the lines below.

_____

_____

_____

_____

- According to **1 John 4:7, 16**, where does love find its source?

_____

God is the only source of agape, the type of love He calls us to. We aren't capable of it without Him. Agape differs greatly from the earthly kinds of love we know. It isn't self-centered, and it always acts in the best interest of others. Agape love responds to God in agreement with His heart, mind, and will because He produces it within you.

Two other characteristics of agape present themselves in Scripture. Agape is always *demonstrated*, and agape *pursues*. Please read **1 John 4:7-12**.

God defines love as obedience to His commands

- What does **verse 8** teach about one who doesn't love (with agape)?

_____

- How did God demonstrate His love in **verse 9**?

_____

- Why did He send His Son?

_____

- *"This is love: not that we loved God, but that he loved us . . ."* (**verse 10**). God loved us first. How did He pursue us?

_____

_____

- Since God *"so loved us,"* what should we also do if He's within us (**verse 11**)?

_____

- According to **verse 12**, what is apparent if we love one another?

_____

Right before His crucifixion, after sharing the Passover meal with His disciples in an upper room, Jesus spoke these words to them:

> *"A new command I give you: Love one another. As I have loved you, so you must love one another. By this all men will know that you are my disciples, if you love one another"*
> (JOHN 13:34-35*).*

Do you seek Jesus and pursue His love, or do you only seek His blessing?

Love is the distinguishing mark of all true disciples of Christ. Can you guess the Greek word for love used in this passage? It's agape, the same word found in 1 John 4:16, *"God is love."* In order for us to love with agape, we must draw it from its source. That's precisely why loving God with all we have must be our first priority.

For us to love as God wills, we must choose to pursue it. We do so by pursuing the source God sent us in a grand demonstration of *His* love. We seek Jesus, *Himself* . . . not His blessing, not His law . . . but *Jesus.*

This, dear one, is what I missed for all those years. I had lots of head knowledge of who Jesus was, but I had never given Him my heart. I am so grateful that our God of love pursues!

I wonder how many times He knocked at the door of my heart, and still I refused to open it. Instead, I dutifully went through the motions of church, settling for my own idea of who He was. I embraced the counterfeit instead of the True. How I praise Him that He offers His mercy anew every day!

Yet the day I finally responded, recognized my sin, received His forgiveness, and asked Him to teach me to love Him, I experienced a longing fulfilled. Love finally opened the door to

His grace, and He has been lavishing me in it ever since!

Above all else, God asks one thing of you. He wants you to love Him. Everything else will begin to flow naturally as a result because of its nature. Love is selfless. Love is demonstrated. Love pursues. *"Love never fails"* (1 Corinthians 13:8).

As we pursue Jesus with a heart set on love, He will begin to move us to demonstrate that love through obedience.

• Return to **John 14** and write **verse 21** on the lines below.

_____

_____

_____

May your love, expressed to Christ through your obedience, open the door to grace.

day 2: CHOSEN FOR A PURPOSE

God has some things to reveal to us today. As we celebrate that Jesus called us to salvation, keep in mind that God always acts according to one, singular purpose: *the completion of His will.*

Ask God to meet you in His Word, and then read **2 Thessalonians 1:3-12.**

- Within this church, two things were happening that caused Paul to rejoice. What were they (**verse 3**)?

  1. _____

  2. _____

- According to **verse 4**, under what conditions was this happening?

  _____

- Because of the evidence revealing itself within this body, what result was Paul certain of for these people (**verse 5**)?

  _____

  _____

- **Verse 6** offers us this glorious assurance: *God is just.* How is the justice of God described?

  _____

  _____

- When are we promised relief from our trouble (**verse 7**)?

  _____

- According to **verse 8**, what two things will Christ punish the ungodly for when He returns?

  1. _____

  2. _____

- How will they be punished (**verse 9**)?

_____

_____

- When He comes to reign, how will Jesus be glorified (**verse 10**)?

_____

Don't miss the significance of verse 10. God's plan is not that Jesus would be glorified *by* us, but rather that He would be glorified *in* us. He seeks not what we do *for* Him, but instead petitions us to allow Him to do a mighty work within and through us.

- Please write **verse 11** on the lines below:

_____

_____

_____

_____

Do you work for Christ, or does Christ work through you?

My heart joins Paul's cry that we all may be counted worthy of His calling as the testing comes.

- By whose power will our purpose be fulfilled (**verse 11**)?

_____

Christ has a work to do in and through you. By His power, He will *"fulfill every good purpose of yours and every **act** prompted by your **faith**."*

- What two things will result in **verse 12**?

1. _____

2. _____

God has a set purpose for your life with specific acts for you to complete that will result in glory. Please read **Ephesians 2:8-10.**

- God offers salvation as a precious and unearned gift. According to **verse 8**, we are saved *by*_____ and *through* _____.

- **Verse 9** clearly states that we are *not* saved by

_____.

However, **verse 10** claims that we are being re-created in Christ Jesus *for* a specific purpose.

- What is that purpose?

_____

- When were those works prepared for us?

_____

I will forever be grateful for the gift of salvation. As I journey the road of life, my shortcomings present themselves with unfortunate frequency, and I am drawn to my knees in gratitude for God's gift of grace. Without grace, I would stand condemned.

God has given so abundantly beyond what we deserve. In answer to our weakness, God has chosen to give *Himself* to us through His Son, offering us the opportunity to overcome.

His gift is so lavish, we spend much time as His church celebrating how very much He loves us. And His grand expression of affection toward us does deserve our praise! But we often become so caught up in proclaiming His love that we lose sight of His purpose. As verse 10 revealed, if we truly belong to Him, there is something He means for us to do.

Before Jesus ever stepped foot on the topsoil of earth, God told His people why He would send Him. Asking His Spirit for understanding, please read **Ezekiel 36:21-23.**

- According to **verse 21**, what was God's concern?

_____

_____

- For whose sake was God going to act (**verse 22**)?

_____

- In **verse 23**, God states His purpose: _"I will show the holiness of my great name."_ How would He do it?

_____

In the verses that follow, God reveals His plan to show Himself holy through His people. Continue reading **verses 24-27.**

- Fill in the blanks according to **verse 24**.

  _"For I will _____ _____ _____ of the nations; I will gather you from all the countries and bring you back into _____ _____ _____."_

- What would He sprinkle on His people (**verse 25**)?

_____

  - What would it do?

  _____

- According to **verse 26**, what two "new" things would God provide for them?

  1. _____

  2. _____

- According to **verse 27**, what will possessing His new Spirit do for us?

_____

_____

Profane: to misuse, defile, to treat with irreverence or contempt, violate the sanctity of

---

"profane." _Dictionary.com_ 2013. http://www.dictionary.reference.com/profane (24 September 2013).

God had a very specific purpose in mind when He authored the plan of salvation. Woven throughout the fabric of His plan ran His desire to reveal His true nature and character to the nations. *"I [will] show myself holy through you before their eyes"* (verse 23).

This time, God's chosen people would no longer profane His name because He Himself would dwell within them. Within the very depths of their beings, He would create a new heart to change their motivations, and possess their spirits with His own. By His Spirit, He would then *"move them to follow."*

Beloved, we are the recipients of that new covenant. As we comply and follow the leadership of His Spirit, we will find ourselves moving in accordance with God's will and completing the works that He prepared for us in advance.

As you begin to operate within the bounds of His purpose for you, you will discover the incomparable joy and satisfaction that can only come from doing what you were made to do. *And your soul will sing.*

Follow Him, dear one. You'll gain everything.

day 3: HALF-HEARTED OBEDIENCE

I recently attended a conference during which the speaker, Lysa TerKeurst, shared a story about her young daughter's misadventure resulting from her eagerness to bake a cake. The girl paraded with great excitement into the kitchen, mixed up the ingredients according to the directions, and poured the batter into the pan. Per her mother's instructions, she allowed her older sister the privilege of sliding the pan into the oven. Then she stood in front of the oven door and watched.

As the minutes ticked on, her impatience grew. Forty minutes is a long time to wait while the oven does its work. The tantalizing aroma of the baking cake began to invade her thoughts and steer her thinking away from the original plan. Surely the cake didn't need forty minutes to be complete. After all, it had risen, and its edges were now kissed with a lovely golden brown. It appeared to be done. It certainly smelled done.

She found her sister and convinced her to comply with her new plan: they would remove the cake from the oven and enjoy its sweet refreshment sooner than anticipated. The last twenty minutes of baking were, in fact, unnecessary. What a blessing! Right?

They removed the cake and set it on the counter to cool, rejoicing over the fast progress they had made. Their glee, however, soon turned to shock and disappointment as only a few minutes into the cooling process, the cake began to collapse upon itself. To their astonishment, all their efforts—their preparation, measuring, stirring, and beating—had yielded them nothing. The work they'd done proved useless, except as a frustrating and difficult life lesson. They had steered from the course set by the author of the recipe, and their work collapsed upon itself, providing no benefit for the ones it was intended to bless.

Welcome to one of the greatest pitfalls in both life and ministry. Our good intentions and our eagerness to see results often cause us to move ahead of God's timing or add things to the mix that were never intended to be there. Like the girls in our illustration,

> **Today's Truth:**
>
> PRIDE GOES BEFORE DESTRUCTION, A HAUGHTY SPIRIT BEFORE A FALL.
> —PROVERBS 16:18

we take matters into our own hands rather than sticking to the instructions provided by the Architect who drew up the blueprint. The results can be disastrous.

As we explore the role of obedience in our daily walk, let's consider two kings, both chosen and anointed by God for leadership over His flock, but whose posture before God brought about very different results. One set his heart on building upon the rock of God's will. The other chose to build according to his own. Please read **Acts 13:21-22**.

Only following God's plan will produce your desired results.

- According to **verse 22**, how did Saul's time of leadership end?

_____

_____

- How did God describe David, Saul's successor?

_____

- What in particular made David a man after God's own heart?

_____

_____

Once again we witness the motivating desire of God's heart compelling Him to action: to see His will lived out on this earth. God removed Israel's first king, Saul, from leadership while He blessed and accepted David, for the simple reason that David desired to be *used* by God to bring about the *will* of God. Saul was more interested in bringing about his own desires, elevating his own name and status.

Please read **1 Samuel 15:1-23**, asking God to open your mind to its truths.

- What instructions did God give to Saul in **verse 3**?

_____

_____

_____

- What did Saul do? List the specific actions he took in **verses 7-9**.

_____

_____

_____

_____

- According to **verse 9**, by what gauge did Saul determine what he would destroy?

_____

_____

  - What does this suggest about the condition of his heart?

  _____

  _____

- How did God respond to Saul's half-hearted obedience (**verse 11**)?

_____

_____

- When Samuel went to find Saul, what did he discover he had been up to (**verse 12**)?

_____

_____

- How did Saul respond to Samuel when he saw him in **verse 13**?

_____

_____

- What was Samuel's reply in **verse 14**?

_____

• How did Saul justify his disobedience in **verses 15 and 21**?

_____

_____

How often do we step outside of God's will with the reasoning that we're doing it *for Him*? We come up with programs and plans that He never authored, and we boldly parade them before Him expecting Him to stamp His approval on our efforts. Our service to Him is, after all, our sacrifice to the Lord. He should be pleased.

• Please write God's response to that thinking from **verse 22** on the lines below.

_____

_____

_____

_____

> *Obedience is better than sacrifice*

God sums up His will for us with these six words, "To **obey** is better than sacrifice." God is not interested in our works, at least not the ones we come up with on our own. What interests Him is whether or not we are living a legacy of faith.

Verse 22 clearly indicates that God examines whether or not we are *"obeying the voice of the Lord."* He is the Word, and He communicates His will continually, watching to see who will listen and participate with Him in His divine plans. Choosing not to heed His instruction and relying on our own understanding becomes a recipe for disaster. Saul found out the hard way. May we learn from his mistakes!

• How did God respond to Saul's arrogance in **verse 23**?

_____

_____

God clearly defines our rebellion as sin, and He sees our arrogance as idolatry. Our participation in either will not be blessed. When we reject His Word to us, choosing instead to follow the path of our own plans, we will find ourselves rejected by His presence, His anointing and His power. And anything we seek to create will simply collapse upon itself. *"Pride goes before destruction, a haughty spirit before a fall"* (Proverbs 16:18).

Take a moment to ask God to show you the condition of your own heart. Whose desires, wishes and commands do you typically exalt each day? Do you live to bring about the will of God in your life, or do you more regularly try to use Him to bring about your own? As Saul discovered, God is not deceived by outward appearances.

Do you seek to live out God's will, or do you try to use Him to bring about your own?

• According to **1 Samuel 16:7**, what does God look at?

_____

God sees straight into the hidden motives of our hearts. He looks for souls who will cooperate with His will and invite Him to reveal His power and blessing. May it be said of you:

"I have chosen [your name], a [wo]man after my own heart. [S]He will do everything I want him [her] to do." ACTS 13:22

day 4: GOD'S UNSTOPPABLE WILL

Before we move on to what God has for us today, let's remind ourselves of two important points from our previous study:

> 1. Without a proper foundation, anything we do will collapse upon itself.
> 2. Obedience is better than sacrifice.

Today's Truth:

THE LORD ALMIGHTY HAS SWORN, "SURELY, AS I HAVE PLANNED, SO IT WILL BE, AND AS I HAVE PURPOSED, SO IT WILL STAND."

—ISAIAH 14:24

The will of God *must* be the foundation of all that we do, whether in our personal lives or in our service to Christ in ministry. God's will is our starting point and our finish line, our link to His blessing and favor, and our gateway to His power and presence. It is our *only* place of safety.

Yesterday we considered two men who were chosen by God to lead His people. We glimpsed into the heart and mind of God as we witnessed through Scripture that God chose David as king over Israel because he was found to have a heart after God's own. God clearly stated the motive behind His choice: "... *he will do everything I want him to do*" (Acts 13:22).

God hand-picked David to rule His people because he loved God with a heart of obedience. David's posture before the Lord would allow God to reveal His splendor and glory throughout Israel.

But what of Saul? Did God make a mistake when He chose him as king over Israel? Let's consider the circumstances surrounding Saul's selection. He was Israel's very first king. Until that time, God had appointed judges and prophets to lead who would communicate with God and reveal His will to the people. Eventually the people decided they wanted more. Please read **1 Samuel 8:4-9.**

- What three reasons did the elders give Samuel for asking him to appoint a king (**verse 5**)?

1. _____

2. _____

3. _____

- How did Samuel respond to their demands in **verse 6**?

_____

_____

- How did the LORD respond to what was happening (**verse 7**)?

_____

_____

_____

God chooses who He will use for His purposes based on the condition of our hearts.

- How were the people rejecting God Himself by asking for a king?

_____

_____

- What had the people been doing continually since their rescue from Egypt (**verse 8**)?

_____

_____

Prior to King Saul, God Himself led His people. He spoke forth His will and gave instructions through prophets, those anointed by God with the ability to hear His voice and communicate back to Him. Obeying those instructions would place God's people securely in His blessing and protection, yet over and over they rejected Him through their mistrust and disobedience.

Now the people determined they would no longer merely submit to the rule of an unseen God. They wanted a king, so the Lord gave them one, but not without giving them a clear warning of what this choice would cost them.

Continue reading **1 Samuel 8:10-22.**

- What did God indicate would be the result of proclaiming a king? List some of their consequences from **verses 10-17**.

_____

_____

_____

_____

- According to **verse 18**, what would be the aftermath of their continuing to follow their own will in this matter?

_____

_____

- How did the people respond in **verse 19**?

_____

Verse 20 breaks my heart as I consider what Israel, and by extension His current church, was designed to be: a peculiar and distinct people, chosen and appointed by God to be uniquely special, different from the rest—a cherished body of believers through whom He would reveal Himself to the world.

And what was Israel's response to such a noteworthy calling? "No thanks. We'd rather be like everybody else." So God gave His chosen people the desire of their hearts, *"Listen to them and give them a king"* (1 Samuel 8:22).

In the same way that God chose David to rule His people because David loved the Lord and would cooperate in bringing about His will for Israel, God chose Saul because he would not. 1 Samuel 9:17 clearly indicates that God hand-picked Saul, *"When Samuel caught sight of Saul, the LORD said to him, 'This is the man I spoke to you about; he will govern my people.'"* Unfortunately, God selected him as the man through whom the people would reap the consequences of their rejection of Him.

We can learn an important lesson from the experience of the Israelites. The will of God cannot be thwarted. Because He is sovereign, one way or another, He will bring about the workings of His plans.

He has, however, given us the choice of whether or not we will participate with Him. We can draw near to Him, seeking His instruction and willingly bend our knees to His will, or we can insist on rejecting His leadership and force our own.

- What does **Galatians 6:7-8** teach us about the result of the path we choose?

_____

_____

_____

- **Verse 9** reveals what benefit of steadfast obedience?

_____

_____

Living by faith expressed through obedience yields a harvest of blessing, displaying the glory of God through supernatural results. Living according to our own will invites the wrath of God and leads to our destruction.

May we wisely choose the path of obedience and blessing.

day 5: A FRESH WORD

G od speaks to us continually. It's no coincidence that John first identifies Jesus in his Gospel as the Word made flesh. God releases His power by doing one seemingly insignificant thing: He speaks. Genesis teaches that He spoke the world into existence, *"Let there be . . .,"* and there was. The mouth of God releases the power of God. Please read **Isaiah 55:8-13**.

- What do **verses 8-9** teach about the thoughts and ways of man?

_____

_____

- What does this indicate about our ability to always see and understand what God is doing?

_____

Our inability to comprehend God's ways leaves us precariously dangling from our uncertain knowledge of God's will for our lives by mere trust. Of this we can be certain: *"The works of his hands are faithful and just; all his precepts are trustworthy. They are steadfast for ever and ever, done in faithfulness and uprightness"* (Psalm 111:7-8). Not only can we believe in the faithfulness of our God, but His precepts—His words of Truth— are unwavering and faithfully given. They are also packed with power.

- To what does God compare His word in **verse 10**?

_____

_____

Today's Truth:

WHAT AGREEMENT IS THERE BETWEEN THE TEMPLE OF GOD AND IDOLS? FOR WE ARE THE TEMPLE OF THE LIVING GOD. AS GOD HAS SAID: "I WILL LIVE WITH THEM AND WALK AMONG THEM, AND I WILL BE THEIR GOD, AND THEY WILL BE MY PEOPLE. THEREFORE, COME OUT FROM THEM AND BE SEPARATE," SAYS THE LORD
—2 CORINTHIANS 6:16-17A

- Please write **verse 11** on the lines below.

_____

_____

_____

- According to **verse 12**, what will be the result of God's Word accomplishing its work in us?

_____

_____

Dear friend, the harvest of joy and peace that we seek will only be found as we know, obey, and treasure the Word of Christ. His word is powerful and will be faithful to accomplish its work, but it will not seep into our marrow through the wood of our bookshelves. We must take time to meet with Him regularly in Scripture.

Look at verse 13. God's Word changes the type of fruit we produce. In this example, pine trees and myrtle will replace thorns and briers. Incidentally, do you know what thorns and briers represent in Scripture? When man first fell into sin through his disobedience to God, he heard these words from the Lord:

Thorns represent the result of sin in Scripture.

> "*Because you listened to your wife and ate from the tree about which I commanded you, 'you must not eat of it,' Cursed is the ground because of you; through painful toil you will eat of it all the days of your life. It will produce thorns and thistles for you, and you will eat the plants of the field*" (GENESIS 3:17-18).

Thorns and thistles represent the consequence of sin. They exist only because man disregarded the Word of the Lord and sought his own way instead.

- Recall what **Proverbs 14:12** teaches about the danger of following our own path and taking the way that seems best to us.

_____

As we saw in Isaiah 55, God's ways are higher than ours. If we act according to what seems logical to us, we will automatically fall short of God's desires. His thoughts and ways are higher. We will not arrive there on our own; we must seek His Word—His instruction to us—and trust His Word through obedience. That's the life of faith God honors. If we don't make the effort to seek His instruction and follow it, our best intentions can prove disastrous.

David discovered that the hard way. This king after God's own heart determined that it was time for the Ark of the Covenant, the dwelling place of God in those days, to be brought to Jerusalem. He had pure motives. He desired to honor God, and he believed moving the ark to Jerusalem would indicate to the people the importance of the presence of God being central to daily life.

Surely God would bless such a desire to honor Him. Please read **2 Samuel 6:1-11**.

- How many men did David bring together for this celebratory march to Jerusalem (**verse 1**)?

_____

- How did they transport the ark (**verse 3**)?

_____

- According to **verse 5**, what were the people doing as the ark was being transported?

_____

- What happened at the threshing floor of Nacon (**verses 6-7**)?

_____

_____

- How did David respond to what happened? List his emotions and actions from **verses 8-10**.

_____

_____

Can you imagine the horrifying shift of emotions that swept through David and the Israelites that day? One minute all of Israel was *"celebrating with all their might before the LORD,"* and in the next moment a man was dead. Imagine their shock and confusion as they questioned how God could have struck Uzzah down. He was only trying to help! David took three months to ponder the matter before he was ready to act again. Please continue reading **verses 12-17**.

- According to **verse 13**, how did David transport the ark this time?

_____

_____

Good intentions can prove disastrous when not submitted to the Lord for His direction.

At first, this may seem to be an insignificant piece of information, but this distinction made all the difference in the eyes of God. David's problem was not what he desired to do for God. His fault lay in the fact that he neglected to inquire of the LORD for instruction as to *how* he should do it.

Consider David's first attempt to transport the ark that ended in disaster: they placed the ark on a new cart. What could have inspired David to try this idea? Perhaps he knew it had been done before.

Before Saul had been anointed king, the Philistines attacked and routed Israel, killing 30,000 soldiers and capturing the ark of God. The ark remained in Philistine territory for seven months, but in every city they brought the ark, God's wrath poured out on the people. The Philistines finally determined the ark must go back to Israel, so they called together their priests and diviners to inquire how they should send it back to its rightful place. This was their answer:

"Now then, get a new cart ready with two cows that have

*calved and have never been yoked. Hitch the cows to the
cart, but take their calves away and pen them up. Take the
ark of the LORD and put it on the cart, and in a chest beside
it put the gold objects you are sending back to him as a guilt
offering. Send it on its way . . ." (1 SAMUEL 6:7-8)*

The ark made it safely into Israelite territory, eventually ending
up at Abinadab's house on the hill, where his son Eleazar was
consecrated to guard the ark (1 Samuel 7:1). There it remained
for years until David determined to bring it to Jerusalem.

*God holds His
children to a
higher standard
than the lost.*

Well, it worked for the Philistines, didn't it? Why not just do
what they did? Why indeed. One huge distinction marked the
Israelites and the Philistines. God did not choose the Philistines
to hear and know His will— that treasured gift He reserved for
Israel. The Philistines could transport the ark in the manner of
their choosing because they didn't know any better. God did
not hold them to the same standard as His children.

• Read **Exodus 25:12-15**. How was the ark to be transported?

_____

_____

• According to **Deuteronomy 10:8**, whose job was it to carry
the ark?

_____

• Skip down to **verses 12-13**. What did God ask of Israel?

_____

_____

_____

• Why did God give Israel commands and decrees (**verse 13**)?

_____

God does not hide His will from us. He will tell us exactly
what He wants. He simply asks that we trust His ways and
seek Him for instruction. Generations had passed between the

giving of the Law to Moses and David's call to be obedient to it. One thing is clear through his experience. We cannot hold out ignorance as an excuse. God has given us everything we need, and He will hold us accountable for how we use what He has given. Had David thought to inquire of the Lord in prayer or even opened the sacred Scriptures, he could have avoided the devastating disaster that claimed a man's life.

How often do we come up with ideas and programs because we know it worked for someone else? Perhaps what we need is a fresh Word. Let's inquire of the Lord and seek His instruction *before* we act. Precious lives are at stake.

Reflections on Week 2

THE NEED FOR AN INNER WORK

Therefore, if anyone is in Christ, he is a new creation;
the old has gone, the new has come!
All this is from God, who reconciled us to himself through Christ . . .

2 CORINTHIANS 5:17-18

day 1 : THE DISTINGUISHING MARK

In **John 11:40**, Jesus asked a profound question of a hurting follower named Martha, whom we are told He loved (verse 5). What did He say to her?

_____

_____

Beloved of God, He asks the same question of you. We who believe are meant to see the glory of God revealed in our lives. And this promise is not just for us. The glory of Jesus Christ resting upon us draws the eyes of a broken world to the allure of its light.

Are people drawn to the presence of Christ in you? Are you distinguishably His? Consistently strewn among the texts of both the Old and New Testaments, we find the reality that God means for His own to be recognizable as His. We're supposed to be able to tell the difference between the redeemed and the lost. Can we? And more importantly, can the world?

In many of our western churches, the lines have somehow blurred. Hypocrisy rears itself with unfortunate frequency, often causing the lost and broken souls Christ means to attract through His body to run emphatically away from our church doors instead of daring to venture inside them. Believers remain broken and bound in oppressive chains and addictions, rather than boldly raising hands lifted in freedom with celebratory praise. Clearly, we are missing something.

Allow Moses to shed some light on our need. Please read **Exodus 33:15-17.**

• What request did Moses make of God in **verse 15**?

_____

_____

- Why (**verse 16**)?

_____

_____

- How did God respond to Moses in **verse 17**?

_____

Oh, that God would have cause to respond to me with those words, "*. . . I am pleased with you and I know you by name.*" The LORD found pleasure in Moses because Moses found pleasure in Him. Verse 11 reveals that "*The LORD would speak to Moses face to face, as a man speaks with his friend.*" Moses spent time in the presence of the LORD, and his experience of that presence produced in him the desire to remain there. The thought of departing from God's presence induced fear, and he pleaded with God not to send them away from Him. In agreement with the character and faithfulness of God, He granted his request.

- How did Moses respond to God's answer in **verse 18**?

_____

May we have the courage to boldly approach the throne of our Creator seeking the revelation of His glory!

Let's take a few moments to consider Moses' initial question for ourselves. If God's *Presence* does not go with us, what will distinguish us from anyone else? The answer, my friend, is *nothing*. Without the presence of God revealing His glory and power in our lives, we remain insignificant to His kingdom. We may intend to bring glory to the Lord who saved us, but if we try to merely imitate His character, we will eventually prove ourselves a fraud. The only way to genuinely reveal Christ to the world is to allow Jesus to make His presence known.

Has He shown Himself in your life? Can you offer testimony of His power at work and share how the touch of Christ's hand in your life left the mark of the miraculous? Beloved, you are meant to *experience* Him.

Many who claim salvation in Jesus Christ miss out on experiencing His *manifest presence*. Being omnipresent, God is

Have you asked Jesus to reveal His glory to you?

everywhere at all times, but there are moments when He makes Himself conspicuous and observable, when He manifests His presence in a tangible way. In those moments, we can see and experience His glory.

During Moses' face-to-face encounters with the Lord, he experienced God's manifest presence in a unique way. Please read **Exodus 34:29-35.**

- Why was Moses' face radiant (**verse 29**)?

_____

- Why did Moses put a veil over his face (**verse 30**)?

_____

- According to **verses 34-35**, when was he careful to remove the veil?

_____

_____

Entering God's presence should alter you!

- What does this suggest about the way we should come into the presence of the Lord?

_____

Simply standing in God's presence altered the appearance of Moses' face enough to be evident to the other Israelites who came in contact with him. They saw the light of God's glory reflected on Moses' face with their own eyes—so much so that it made them a bit uncomfortable.

This story of Moses is referenced again in the New Testament, linking Moses' experience with that of the New Covenant believer. Please read **2 Corinthians 3:7-17,** asking God to give you understanding of His Word.

- According to **verse 7**, what caused Moses' radiant face?

_____

- How is the Old Testament glory described (**verses 7, 11, 13**)?

_____

The "*ministry that brought death, which was engraved in letters on stone*" refers to the giving of the law, specifically the Ten Commandments. On this side of the cross, Christ has released us from our bondage to the law and has given us instead the gift of His Spirit.

- How should the glory revealed under this new covenant compare to the glory Moses and the Israelites experienced under the first one (**verses 8- 9**)?

_____

- How does the glory of the New Covenant differ?
    - **Verse 9**

    _____

    - **Verse 11**

    _____

    - **Verses 13, 18**

    _____

- The Spirit of the Lord reveals the glory of the Lord. According to **verse 17**, what always accompanies the presence of the Spirit?

_____

- Fill in the blanks for **verse 18**.

    "*And we, who with _____ _____ all _____ the Lord's glory, are being _____ into his likeness with _____-_____ glory, which comes from_____ _____, who is the Spirit.*"

Dear one, you are meant to reflect the glory of the Lord! Christ stretched out His arms on a cross to tear the veil separating you from God's presence. No longer must you stand behind a curtain; you've been invited to enter in.

Even more astonishing is God's gift poured out after the cross. Not only can the redeemed enter His presence without fear, but He has chosen to allow His *Presence* to enter us! And that presence inside us desires to transform us into the very likeness of Christ. Notice what accompanies that transformation: *ever-increasing glory*!

Jesus intends to reveal God's glory, and He's chosen to do it through you. God did not design His church to merely imitate Christ's behavior. We have been chosen to allow Jesus to disclose Himself in us with ever-increasing glory.

Will you, like Moses, remain in His presence so that others may see Him in you?

day 2: FILLED TO OVERFLOWING

Yesterday we celebrated the truth that God seeks to reveal His glory. He isn't hiding. He desires to make His presence known in each of our lives, and He's looking for hearts that will cooperate. Today we will discover how the *indwelling* presence of the Holy Spirit becomes the *visible* presence of the Holy Spirit.

Earlier in our study, we briefly explored Jesus' promise to His disciples that He would send a Counselor, the Holy Spirit. This Counselor would guide His followers, teaching them truth and lighting the path for each of their journeys. Let's explore some significant information surrounding the Spirit's arrival. Please read **John 7:37-39.**

- According to **verse 38**, what will happen to anyone who believes in Jesus?

_____

  - Note the present, active participle of the verb "believes." For streams of living water to presently and continually flow, we must presently, continually, and actively believe.

- How did Jesus further clarify the living water in **verse 39**?

_____

  - Why had He been unable to give them the Spirit up to that point?

_____

Now let's fast forward to another scene, where Scripture allows us to glimpse an encounter between Jesus and His disciples after His death and resurrection. Please read **John 20:19-22,** asking God for understanding.

> *Today's Truth:*
>
> "'IN THE LAST DAYS, GOD SAYS, I WILL POUR OUT MY SPIRIT ON ALL PEOPLE. YOUR SONS AND DAUGHTERS WILL PROPHESY, YOUR YOUNG MEN WILL SEE VISIONS, YOUR OLD MEN WILL DREAM DREAMS.'"
> —ACTS 2:17

- What had just taken place that would cause the disciples to be *"together, with the doors locked for fear of the Jews"*?

_____

- What happened while they were gathered there (**verse 19**)?

_____

- How did Jesus assure them of who He was (**verse 20**)?

_____

  - How did they respond?

_____

- What did He tell them in **verse 21**?

_____

_____

- List the two things Jesus did in **verse 22**.

  1. _____

  2. _____

- According to **Isaiah 55:11**, what happens when God speaks?

_____

_____

We have just witnessed a wonderful moment in history: the giving of the Holy Spirit to the very first believers. It reminds me of the first time God gave man a spirit in Genesis 2:7, *"the LORD God formed the man from the dust of the ground and **breathed into his nostrils** the breath of life, and the man **became a living being**"* (emphasis mine). Unfortunately, man's choice to sin caused him to return to the dust he came from (Genesis 3:19), but Christ's work on the cross released him from sin's curse and opened the way for man to once again *"become a living being."* And then, in a private room behind locked doors, Jesus imparted to His first precious followers the breath of eternal life.

Please read **Ephesians 1:11-14.**

• God works out everything according to what (**verse 11**)?

_____

• What are we who hope in Christ to be (**verse 12**)?

_____

• According to **verse 13**, when do we become *"included in Christ"*?

_____

• At what time are we marked with the seal of the Holy Spirit?

_____

• What does the seal of the Holy Spirit do (**verse 14**)?

_____

Jesus seals us with His Holy Spirit the moment we believe.

We become *"included in Christ"* the moment we believe. As we repent of our sin, abandon our former lives, and confess His lordship over us in belief, the Holy Spirit immediately takes up residence in our hearts to seal our position in His kingdom (Acts 2:38, Romans 10:9-10).

Jesus' first disciples left everything to follow Him. Through their experiences with the Son of Man, they believed with certainty that Jesus was the promised Messiah, the Son of God, and they were ready to commit to live according to His will. And now that Christ had accomplished His work, the Spirit could be given. In John 20:22, speaking the words, *"Receive the Holy Spirit,"* and breathing on them the breath of life, Jesus sealed His disciples as His own by the giving of His Spirit. They were marked with the deposit that would guarantee their inheritance in His kingdom, and nothing could snatch them out of His hands.

This gift to them was only the beginning. Before Jesus ascended into heaven, He gave them some further instructions. Please read **Acts 1:1-5.**

- What command did Jesus give His disciples in **verse 4**?

_____

_____

- How did Jesus describe the gift they would receive from the Father in **verse 5**?

_____

    - What does the word "baptize" mean?

_____

- According to **verse 8**, what accompanies the baptism of the Holy Spirit?

_____

Acts 2:1-4 describes the giving of this gift.

- Fill in the blanks according to **verse 4**.

"All of them were _____
with the Holy Spirit and began to speak in other tongues as
the Spirit _____*them."*

Before Pentecost, Jesus' disciples were *sealed* by the Spirit. After Pentecost, they were *filled* with the Spirit, and with this filling came a demonstration of supernatural power.

Scholars agree that the events at Pentecost mark the establishment of the church. God designed the church, not as a building, but as individuals housing the very Spirit of Christ. These believers would act as His visible body, moving in one accord with His will to reveal His glory to a lost world.

Christ's church began with an awesome demonstration of power. The sound of a rushing wind came from heaven and filled the house, leaving no doubt as to the source of this great gift. Tongues of fire separated and came to rest on each of them. Ordinary men became extraordinary men, as the Spirit of Christ overtook the boundaries of human thought and ability and enabled them to preach the Gospel to the gathered masses in their own individual languages! Onlookers heard the Word spoken to them in their own tongue, and were able to understand and believe. God established His church with a grand display of what He designed it to be—human vessels fully submitted to the control and power of His Spirit.

Salvation itself requires only the seal of the Holy Spirit upon our hearts. But if we're going to actually **be** the church, a living reflection of the beauty, holiness and love of Christ that shines His glory to the lost, we cannot simply *possess* His Spirit. We must be *filled* with it. We must learn to yield to His authority in our lives and allow His presence to penetrate every area of our hearts, minds and bodies. Only as we surrender to Him, complying with His Spirit as He seeks to fully possess and fill us, will we allow Christ to be seen.

End today's lesson with a prayer of surrender to your Savior. Relinquish control of your thoughts, will, and emotions to the only One who can be trusted to use them wisely. Ask Him to show you anything hidden deep within you that's keeping you from really letting go.

I offer you one, small suggestion. You may want to meet Him on your knees.

God's design for the church: human vessels fully submitted to the control and power of the Holy Spirit under the leadership of Jesus.

day 3: RESULTS OF THE FILLING

W e spend so much of our lives feeling empty, hungering and thirsting after some means to satisfy the aching void deep within. Beloved, you were not designed to remain empty. God means for you to be filled. *"Open wide your mouth and I will fill it"* (Psalm 81:10). Please read **Ephesians 3:16-19**.

- What is available to us through the Spirit (**verse 16**)?

_____

- What does God desire that we be rooted and established in (**verse 17**)?

_____

- According to **verse 19**, what occurs when we *"know this love that surpasses knowledge?"*

_____

Dear one, God desires to fill us with the complete measure of Himself! In accordance with this purpose, He sent us Jesus, *"For God was pleased to have all his fullness dwell in him, and through him to reconcile to himself all things, whether things on earth or things in heaven, by making peace through his blood, shed on a cross"* (Colossians 1:19-20).

God allowed all His fullness to dwell within the person of His Son, that through Him, His fullness might also dwell within us. Please read **Ephesians 1:15-23**.

- On behalf of his Ephesian brothers, what did Paul ask God for in **verse 17**?

_____

  - For what purpose?

_____

- In **verse 18**, Paul prayed for the lifting of deception's veil. He wanted their hearts to be enlightened to know what?

_____

- What is available to all who believe (**verse 19**)?

_____

- Where has Christ been seated since the resurrection (**verse 20**)?

_____

- According to **verse 22**, what has been placed under His feet?

_____

  - Christ is head over what in particular?

  _____

- How is the body of Christ described in **verse 23**?

_____

_____

Jesus will fill us with His Spirit to the extent that we yield to His authority. We don't need any more of His Spirit to be filled; His Spirit needs more of us.

Did you know that by Christ's very nature, He fills all things in every way? Is He filling you? Comparing Ephesians 1:22-23 with Colossians 2:9-10 yields this common denominator: Scripture links Christ's *authority* with the church's experience of His fullness. We will be filled by Him only to the extent that we yield to Him.

Yesterday, we witnessed a distinction between one who merely houses the presence of the Holy Spirit and one who is filled by Him. Our goal for the remainder of this week will be to discover what we must do to allow this filling to occur, but today we will finish by celebrating some of what Scripture teaches will result when we allow the Spirit of Christ to fill us.

In the face of great persecution, a group of believers in the early church gathered together to make a request of the Lord. Please read **Acts 4:29-31**.

- What did these believers ask of God in **verse 29**?

_____

_____

- What 3 things happened as a result of their prayer (**verse 31**)?

1. _____

2. _____

3. _____

As we surrender to the filling of the Spirit, we become transformed into Christ's image and empowered beyond our own capabilities.

Oh, that we would once again become a church so unified in heart and purpose that our prayers would shake the walls of our meeting houses! They asked and God answered, and *none* were excluded from His gift. Notice the text says *all* of them were filled with the Spirit, and that filling brought about the result they had asked for. They all *"spoke the word of God boldly."*

How often we are tempted to think that the role of boldly speaking Truth is reserved for pastors and evangelists. God's Word to us indicates otherwise. We have all that we need to proclaim His Word because the Word lives within us. And as we call upon Him to fill our minds and hearts and enable us with His power, just like He did for those early disciples, He will fill us with His presence and bestow upon us an ability to be smarter than we are.

- According to **John 14:26**, what will the Holy Spirit do?

_____

- What promise did Jesus give in **Luke 12:11-12**?

_____

_____

Dear one, we struggle with our ability to step out in boldness because we have been relying on our own meager ability! Give Jesus the opportunity to show Himself through you. Ask Him to fill your mind and anoint your tongue that He may use you to speak boldly and bring glory to His name!

Let's close our time together today by looking at a man who Scripture describes as being *"full of faith and of the Holy Spirit"* (Acts 6:5). Please read **Acts 6:8-15.**

- According to **verse 8**, what was Stephen also filled with?

_____

- What happened when men argued in opposition to Stephen (**verse 10**)?

_____

- Was Stephen a preacher? See **verses 2-5**. What was Stephen's role in the church?

_____

- What outward manifestation of God's presence did Stephen display in **verse 15**?

_____

Ecclesiastes 8:1 teaches, *"Wisdom brightens a man's face and changes its hard appearance."* Just as the Israelites in Moses' day saw the glory of the LORD reflected radiantly upon his face after time spent in God's presence, the crowd of onlookers at Stephen's trial saw visible evidence of the Lord on him. Stephen offers a New Testament example of the all-surpassing glory of the New Covenant reflected upon his unveiled face (2 Cor. 3:7-18)!

The next 53 verses of **Acts 7** share a powerful sermon from the mouth of Stephen, a man whose job in ministry was overseeing the distribution of food. Just like his Lord and Savior, his message was not well received. Please read **verses 54-60.**

- How did the people respond in **verse 54**?

_____

- How is Stephen described in **verse 55**?

_____

- What two things did his condition allow him to see?

    1. _____

    2. _____

Enraged, the crowd dragged him out of the city and began to stone him.

- What was his response in **verses 59-60**?

_____

_____

Stephen's words pierce my heart as they so closely echo the ones Jesus Himself cried out to the Father on the day of His execution. And on this day, as the Spirit within him lifted his gaze to the heavens and opened his eyes to see, Stephen witnessed Christ, not seated at the right hand of the Father, but on His feet, ready to welcome him into paradise. As the Spirit filled him with His presence, fear held no grip on Stephen's heart. Instead, love flooded his being, his last words petitioning Christ on behalf of his attackers.

We find it hard to imagine those words escaping our lips if we found ourselves in the same circumstance. And we're probably right. Standing amidst such hatred simply as ourselves, we would be overcome. But Stephen did not stand before his accusers as a mere man. The Spirit of Christ filled him, flooding him with grace and love, and empowered him to achieve what he could not attain in his own strength. And even amidst terrible torment, he exited this life with joy in the One he knew had saved him.

The secret to becoming all that God has called us to be is surrender. In ourselves we don't have the power to love our enemies, turn the other cheek, or even reveal God's glory. But when we yield to the power and presence of the Holy Spirit within us and allow Him to *fill* us, that which is impossible becomes possible, and the ordinary becomes the extraordinary.

And he will stand, for the Lord is able to make him stand.
ROMANS 14:4

day 4: "Walk Before Me And Be Blameless"

As we begin today's lesson, I'd like to remind you of a promise found in Peter's second epistle. Please read **2 Peter 1:3-4.**

- According to **verse 3**, what has the divine power of Jesus bestowed to us through the salvation given us?

_____

  - How does this provision come to us?

  _____

- What two things do these great and precious promises allow us to do (**verse 4**)?

  1. _____

  2. _____

As we explore the Scriptures God has for us today, keep these truths in the forefront of your mind. Jesus' power provides us with *"everything we need for life and godliness."* You, dear one, lack nothing necessary to live a godly life. Divine power resides in you through your knowledge of Jesus Christ, giving you the awesome privilege and ability to participate in His divine nature and escape the corruption of the world. May you *believe* His promise and allow its truth to take root in the depths of your soul.

We have been examining God's call to each of us to live a life of faith. Scripture records Abraham as the first to answer that call and has set him before us as our model and example, naming him the father of us all (Romans 4:16). Now let's consider a specific command God gave to Abraham that He asks of us as well. Please read **Genesis 17:1.**

- What did God tell Abraham to do?

_____

I realize I may have lost you right there. Blamelessness seems too difficult a thing. In our minds, we equate that word blameless with "perfect," and the realization that we cannot be perfect often leads us to disregard the command altogether. God could not possibly have been serious about that, right? Yet there it is, written and preserved in Holy Scripture, begging our obedience.

In case you're thinking that particular Scripture was meant only for Abraham and can't be applied to us, let's check the New Testament.

- According to **1 Thessalonians 3:13**, in what condition does God hope to find us when Jesus returns in glory?

_____

There's no getting around God's call to blamelessness. Since He obviously desires it of us, and our aim as one of His own should be to please Him, we must learn what it means.

What does God mean when He asks us to be found blameless? Rather than defining it based on our own understanding, let's allow God to show us His definition. Please read **Psalm 19:13**.

Blameless does not equal perfect.

- Under what two conditions will we be found blameless and innocent of great transgression?

  1. _____

  2. _____

Dear one, we can be redeemed children of God and yet not be found blameless by Him upon Christ's return. From the moment of our salvation, our belief in Jesus will assure our entrance into heaven, but Scripture is clear that we will all one day stand before Christ to give an accounting for the lives we lived while claiming the safety and blessing of His Name. Read **2 Corinthians 5:9-10**.

- According to **verse 9**, what should be our goal?

_____

- What will happen at the judgment seat of Christ?

_____

_____

Receiving what is *due us "for the things done while in the body"* is a sobering thought. May we, like the Apostle Paul, *"make it our goal to please him."* We saw earlier that God wills for us to be found blameless. According to Psalm 19:13, in order for God to view us as innocent and blameless, two things must be true.

> **We must keep ourselves from *willful* sin, and we must not allow any sin to rule and reign over us.**

Friend, the ultimate penalty for our sin has been paid. Christ's blood spilled on our behalf and applied to us as we believe in Him, forever releases us from the curse of death and hell that accompanies our sin. However, our choice to continue to sin once purchased and redeemed is not without cost.

- According to **Isaiah 57:17**, what is one punishment we may reap upon ourselves if we willfully choose to continue sinning?

_____

  - Based on this verse, what is God's goal in hiding His face?

_____

One who is blameless submits to only one authority: Jesus.

To bring us to repentance and incite us to return to Him, God will hide His face from those who choose to continue to live in their own willful ways. Please read **Isaiah 59:1-2**.

- What does **verse 1** teach about God's reach in our circumstances?

_____

_____

• According to **verse 2**, what do our iniquities do to us?

_____

_____

Choosing to continue in sin separates us from God.

Willful sin keeps our requests to God from reaching His ears. Notice Scripture doesn't say He *cannot* hear; it says He *will* not. Psalm 18:41 adds, _"They cried for help, but there was no one to save them—to the LORD, but He did not answer."_

Our cries for help will not be heard by our holy God while we willfully choose to embrace sin. You may be tempted to argue that the grace of God poured out through Christ's cross negates this principle for New Covenant believers. However, we find this Old Testament principle repeated in the New Testament.

• Please write **John 9:31** on the lines below.

_____

_____

God's words from Malachi 3:6 come to mind, _"I the LORD do not change."_

We want God to hear our cries. List what happened in each of the following Scriptures as a result of God hearing.

• **Genesis 21:17-19**

_____

_____

_____

• **2 Samuel 22:7, 17-18**

_____

_____

Celebrate the biblical principle that when God "hears," He moves on behalf of those He has heard! If we desire to see the glory of God revealed in our lives as He demonstrates that He is *for us*, we need to position ourselves to be heard by Him.

We have already seen through Scripture that this process will involve the removal of willful sin. **2 Chronicles 7:14** lists four things God's people must do to be heard. What are they?

1. _____

2. _____

3. _____

4. _____

• What two things will God do once He hears?

1. _____

2. _____

Precious one, God desires to both hear and heal. In fact, God's eagerness to cleanse us and free us from our sin flows from His desire to draw near and disclose Himself to us. He calls you to blamelessness so He can reveal Himself fully in your life.

We will not be free from sin's influence until Christ returns, but through Him we now have a choice over whether or not we give into it. Turn from the power of willful sin and ask Jesus to empower you to obedience. Draw on His strength in your weakness. Sin is already a defeated foe! Allow Jesus to defeat it in you.

God calls you to be blameless so He can reveal Himself fully in your life.

day 5: SANCTIFIED BY BLOOD

May God himself, the God of peace, sanctify you through and through. May your whole spirit, soul and body be kept blameless at the coming of our Lord Jesus Christ.

1 THESSALONIANS 5:23

Today's Truth:

THOSE WHO BELONG TO CHRIST JESUS HAVE CRUCIFIED THE FLESH WITH ITS PASSIONS AND DESIRES.

—GALATIANS 5:24

Yesterday we considered God's call to walk before Him in blamelessness. Our opening Scripture today reminds us that Christ seeks to see us blameless at His return. There is but one path to attain that end. You must allow *"God himself"* to *"sanctify you through and through."*

As members of Christ's body, we were sanctified and freed from sin's penalty the moment we confessed our belief in Jesus as Lord and entered into His kingdom. Christ's work in our lives, however, does not cease at that moment—it begins. God intends our salvation to be the first step in our sanctification process, but two more stages remain.

Consider the three stages of our sanctification.

1. The first stage—**salvation**—frees us from the *penalty* of sin.
2. The second stage—**ongoing sanctification**—frees us from the *power* of sin in our lives.
3. The final stage—**complete sanctification**—occurs upon death or Christ's return and will free us from the very *presence* of sin.

If you belong to Jesus, He has already freed you from sin's ultimate consequence. Now He desires to release you from its power!

Let's revisit **Psalm 19:13**. Under what two conditions will we be found blameless and innocent of great transgression?

1. _____

2. _____

We have already examined some of the biblical consequences of willfully choosing to sin once redeemed. Now we will consider the second aspect of God's call to blamelessness. We must not allow sin to rule and reign.

Please read **Romans 6:8-14**, asking God for understanding of His Word.

- According to **verse 8**, under what condition will we live with Christ?

_____

- What did Christ gain when He rose from the dead (**verse 9**)?

_____

How you live matters.

- What was Christ dying to when He died (**verse 10**)?

_____

- To whom does He now live?_____

- In Christ, what are we also to die to (**verse 11**)?

_____

- What command are we given in **verse 12**?

_____

_____

Verse 13 reminds us that as believers, we now have a choice. We can either continue to offer ourselves in slavery to sin, or we can offer ourselves to God as *"instruments of righteousness."*

- What does **verse 14** reveal as the result of grace?

_____

Dear one, I believe grace is one of the most misunderstood concepts in Scripture. Some have twisted its meaning to say that because of grace, we can do whatever we want. We're no longer bound to the law, which means we're free to do as we please without consequence. We're already forgiven!

- What was Paul's response to that line of thinking in **verse 15?**

_____

I pray you will heed Scripture's counsel. Jude 4 warns of condemned men who have secretly slipped in among the body, *"godless men who change the grace of our God into a license for immorality and deny Jesus Christ our only Sovereign and Lord."* Verse 13 cautions that these men *"are wild waves of the sea, foaming up their shame; wandering stars, for whom blackest darkness has been reserved forever."*

God's grace poured out to us through Jesus does not offer us free license to sin. Rather, grace dispenses the power to do what we were not capable of under the law. It enables us to *overcome sin's rule* (Romans 6:14) and live out our days in glorious freedom! Grace provides the opportunity to live a righteous life.

Friend, the grace offered through Christ actually calls us to a *higher* standard of living. Consider Jesus' words in **Matthew 5:17-20.**

- According to **verse 17**, what did Jesus come to do?

_____

- How should our righteousness compare to that of the Pharisees (**verse 20**)?

_____

Jesus continued His sermon with some astonishing statements. After reminding the crowd of the law's command to abstain from murder, Christ declared that God's people would now be judged merely for harboring anger toward their brother (verse 22). The law condemned man for adultery. Under grace, Jesus claimed, *"But I tell you that anyone who looks at a woman lustfully has already committed adultery with her in his heart"* (verse 28). The law commanded us to love our neighbors, but grace insists we love our enemies as well (verses 43-44).

Grace, dear one, holds us to a higher standard. Judgment moves beyond the outer action to the heart from which it

> *For sin shall no longer be your master, because you are not under the law, but under grace.*
>
> —ROMANS 6:14

springs. Why? Because a perfect, holy, and righteous God now resides within us, and His power enables us to cut off sin at its source. Now, we are without excuse.

As believers, we have *one* Sovereign and Lord. Our allegiance is to one Master, who is righteousness itself. Jesus must be permitted to take His place as Lord and Master of our hearts. For Him to do so, we must reject any other ruling authority.

- According to **Galatians 5:1**, why did Jesus come?

_____

- Whose job is it to see that we as believers don't succumb to a yoke of slavery?

_____

The chains of sin wear many disguises. Pride passes itself off as insecurity. Impatience springs from a chain of self-centeredness. Bitterness is linked to our refusal to forgive. Untreated wounds put up barriers in our lives that we don't even recognize as chains, and the protective walls we build around our hearts keep us from the love God desires to lavish on us and through us.

Grace holds us to a higher standard of righteousness than the law.

Christ traveled the road to the cross to purchase your freedom. He endured the beating and taunting of His accusers. He allowed the flogger's whip to strip flesh from His back and permitted mocking guards to beat a crown of thorns into His head. Blood dripped from the nails in His hands and feet, bathing the ground beneath the cross with the life-flow of our Savior. Every drop of blood spilled that day poured out from Jesus toward one end: to purchase your freedom from sin's chains. Will you so carelessly allow them to remain?

Jesus means to fill your heart, mind, and body with Himself. Any part of you still enslaved to your sin nature remains a place His Spirit doesn't fill. Strongholds of sin quench the work of the Spirit and work against the completion of God's will. Only as you reject sin's rule and allow Jesus to reign within your heart will you begin to take on His righteousness as your own. The release of your chains will usher in the revelation of His glory!

Please read **John 8:31-36**, asking God to give you understanding of His Word.

• What specific group did Jesus address in **verse 31**?

_____

    • How did Jesus distinguish which ones were really true disciples?

    _____

• According to **verse 32**, what sets us free from our chains?

_____

• What did Jesus teach about sin in **verse 34**?

Jesus died to _____

conquer the

power of sin   • What promise do we have through the Son (**verse 36**)?

in your life.   _____

Dear one, Jesus paid an exorbitant price for your redemption. He exchanged His precious life to ransom you from sin's chains. Let's not waste a single drop of the blood Christ shed.

> *This is what God the LORD says—*
> *He who created the heavens and stretched them out, Who spread out*
> *the earth and all that comes out of it,*
> *Who gives breath to its people, and life to those who walk on it: "I,*
> *the LORD, have called you in righteousness;*
> *I will take hold of your hand;*
> *I will keep you and will make you to be a covenant for the people*
> *And a light for the Gentiles,*
> *To open eyes that are blind, To free captives from prison*
> *And to release from the dungeon those who sit in darkness.*
> *I am the LORD; that is my name!*
> *I will not give my glory to another or my praise to idols."*
> ISAIAH 42:5-8

Beloved, may your heart cry out to the Lord,

"I run in the path of your commands, for you have set my heart free."
PSALM 119:32

Reflections on Week 3

_____

_____

_____

_____

_____

_____

_____

_____

_____

_____

_____

_____

_____

_____

_____

_____

_____

_____

BECOME A LIVING STONE

See to it that you do not refuse him who speaks . . .
"Once more I will shake not only the earth but also the heavens."
The words 'once more' indicate the removing of what can be shaken— that
is, created things—so that what cannot be shaken may remain.

HEBREWS 12:25-27

day 1 : WASTED EFFORTS

You're on the home stretch, my friend! I pray that the truths we've discovered together in God's Word will be planted deep within the soil of your heart, producing the proper harvest in God's perfect time. May the Spirit cultivate and grow that which you have obediently sown!

Today we cast our gaze upon a defining moment in our history, a time when God intervened to decisively demonstrate that the will of man will not overcome His own. Please read **Genesis 11:1-9**, asking God to reveal fresh truths hidden within the text.

- According to **verse 4**, what two goals did the people mean to achieve by building *"a tower that reaches to the heavens"*?

    1. _____

    2. _____

Once again, our human need for self-promotion rears its ugly head. Man repeatedly insists on seeking his own glory instead of seeking to glorify God. We will battle the powerful pull of our own natures until Christ returns, but in the meantime, we have this hope: *"In all these things we are more than conquerors through him who loved us"* (Romans 8:37). Amen!

We can't fully understand the significance of their second goal without taking a peek at the events leading up to their decision to build this city. If you glance at the headings in your Bible, you'll notice this gathering of people on a plain in Shinar occurred on the heels of the great flood. God was repopulating the earth after He had wiped out its occupants for their rebellion, and Genesis 9:1 clearly reveals God's intentions for Noah and his sons, those He had chosen to redeem.

- What command did God give to Noah and his offspring in **Genesis 9:1**?

_____

God had a purpose in His salvation of the few, and in keeping with that purpose, He instructed those who remained to *"fill the earth."* With His command came the promise of provision.

• What promise did God make in **verse 2**?

_____

_____

Man consistently chooses to trust his own ways rather than the God who created him.

Consider for a moment the motive that often causes people to unite: we find strength and safety in numbers. Our abilities to protect and provide multiply as our numbers multiply.

Yet God commanded them to scatter. When He did, He offered them an invitation to believe, to put their trust in Him as their Redeemer. Essentially, He asked them not to rely on their own abilities to protect and provide for one another, but rather to trust and rely on Him.

He addressed their need for protection, assuring them that *"the fear and dread of you will fall upon the beasts of the earth . . . upon every creature that moves along the ground . . . they are given into your hands."* He also made a promise of provision, telling them, *"Everything that lives and moves will be food for you. Just as I gave you the green plants, I now give you everything"* (Genesis 9:3).

Unfortunately, due to the reigning rule of sin, man consistently chooses to trust himself rather than the God who created him. Within a few generations of receiving the miraculous salvation of God in the face of utter destruction, seeds of rebellion, the very thing that caused God to destroy the earth by flood and begin again, took root and grew within the hearts of man.

Contrast God's instructions to Noah with their reason for building the tower in **Genesis 11:4.**

• What exactly did they rebel against?

_____

The flesh wants what it wants. That's precisely why we will not stand for long without allowing God to reconstruct our heart and rid it of sin. Like the little girl's cake in our earlier illustration, our own weak center will soon cause us to collapse upon ourselves no matter how good our intentions when we began.

We must purposefully draw near to God each day, choosing to live in the light of His presence and according to His will, or we will soon find ourselves seeking to exalt our own names instead of The Name. Pride's ascension within our hearts will leave us standing on very shaky ground.

Verse 3 reveals another significant piece of information. Fill in the blanks to complete the verse:

"Come, let's make bricks and bake them thoroughly." They used _____ *instead of* _____. . ."

- List anything you can think of that distinguishes brick from stone.

_____

_____

Brick-Maker: striving in your own strength to create works you design.

The people of the earth came together in rebellion against the will of God. They determined to make a name for themselves instead of allowing God to make a name for Himself through them. How would they accomplish this? By building a tower reaching to the heavens for all to see. What would they use to build this tower? Bricks made by their own hands, rather than stone formed by the hand of God.

Dear one, how often do we attempt to build towers reaching to the heavens for all to see? Sometimes we don't even recognize the desire to make a name for ourselves. Our deceitful hearts will tell us we're doing it for Jesus, and we boldly claim we're building the tower to exalt His name. Yet the tower we build is not comprised of stones cut from the hand of God. Instead we labor and toil to build with bricks made by our own.

We've become quite good at making bricks. Some of those bricks bear the labels of righteous traits we try diligently to produce in our own lives. Some of them are works of service we present to the Lord in an attempt to earn His approval. Others are works we do for ourselves to garner the approval of man. Either way, they're all bricks . . . and all meaningless because we're the ones producing them.

Are you weary, friend? All our striving and brick-making has left us exhausted. Dear one, the body of Christ isn't meant for wearisome toil. Please read **Matthew 11:28-30**.

• According to **verse 28**, what does Jesus offer the weary and burdened?

_____

• How do we find it? List the two instructions Jesus gives in **verse 29**.

1. _____

2. _____

"For my yoke is easy and my burden is light" (verse 30). When we take the yoke of Christ's leadership upon us and allow Him the right to lead and steer us in the direction of the Father's will, our burden becomes light. We escape the wearisome heavy labor of making our own bricks, and He takes on the heavy lifting! He begins to move and maneuver circumstances and people according to His plan. Rather than working feverishly to make things happen, we get to sit back and revel in the glory of watching Him move!

Jesus didn't call you to be a brick-maker. He called you to become a living stone. Please read **1 Peter 2:4-6**.

Living Stone: led and empowered by the Holy Spirit to fulfill God's purpose.

• What command are we given in **verse 4**?

_____

Remember Jesus' command in Matthew 11:28? *"**Come to me, all you who are weary and burdened, and I will give you rest.**"* Our "rest" will only come to us as we commit to draw near.

• What happens as we come to Him, according to **1 Peter 2:5**?

_____

_____

_____

Dear one, only as we allow Jesus to mold us by His power into a living stone do our offerings to the Father become *"spiritual sacrifices **acceptable** to God through Jesus Christ"* (verse 5, emphasis mine).

God Himself is the builder, the grand architect constructing a spiritual house that reaches to the heavens, and He does this through His Son. His is the Name worthy of glory. His work, and His alone, will stand at the end of days.

Glory belongs to Jesus, not man. But one of the wonderful aspects of His character is that when we choose to live for His glory instead of our own, He extends His glory to us, *". . . that the name of our Lord Jesus may be glorified in you, and **you in him**"* (2 Thessalonians 1:12, emphasis mine).

- According to **2 Thessalonians 2:14**, what benefit do we gain by answering His call?

_____

_____

_____

Submit yourself to the Lord of Glory. Allow Him to shape you and place you precisely in His purpose for you. You will bask in the overflow of His glory as He builds, and partake of your share when He returns!

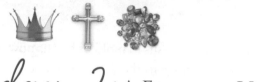

day 2: A Fruitful Vineyard

D o you find any measure of relief from the realization that it isn't your job to build Christ's church? That's His job! He already sees the finished project and knows exactly what needs to take place to bring it to completion. It's not our role to figure out how to build it for Him. Such posture indicates pride and removes us from His presence and power. Our role is to simply allow Him to use us as the tools through whom *He* builds.

- What command does God give us in **Psalm 46:10**?

_____

- According to this verse, what goal does He seek to achieve?

_____

Dear one, building according to our own works exalts *us*, not the Lord of glory. We exalt God when we obey Psalm 46:10; we must *be still*, and we must know that *He* is God. This Scripture doesn't teach that we're never to do anything. Rather, it cautions us to quiet ourselves, draw near to the Living Word, and listen until we've heard from on high. Then, we must obediently take action in faith.

Please read **John 15:1-8**, asking God to give you understanding of His Word.

- Jesus speaks as the *"I am"* in this passage. What is His role, according to **verse 1**?

_____

- What is the Father's role? _____

- What two things does the Father do as the gardener (**verse 2**)?

1. _____

2. _____

- What has made the hearers "clean," according to **verse 3**?

_____

- What does **verse 4** teach about our ability to bear fruit?

_____

- Fill in the blanks, according to **verse 5**.

   "I am the_____; you are the _____.

   If a man_____in me and I in him, he

   will   _____; apart

   from me, _____."

- To what does Jesus compare one who does not "remain in Him" (**verse 6**)?

_____

   - What happens to such a branch?

   _____

- Contemplate our definition of the wise man who builds upon the rock (Matthew 7:24): one who *hears* Jesus' words and puts them into practice. What do you think it means to "remain in Him"?

_____

- Under what two conditions are we guaranteed the promise of **verse 7**, *"ask whatever you wish, and it will be given you"*?

   1. _____

   2. _____

- What brings the Father glory (**verse 8**)?

_____

Our fruit-bearing reveals us as authentic disciples of Christ. *"Thus, by their fruit you will recognize them"* (Matthew 7:20). Note the word Jesus uses to describe our bounty: *much* fruit.

The glory of God reveals itself as we allow Him to produce abundant fruit in and through us. This fruit can be grown only through our attachment to the one true vine, Jesus. Consider Christ's words in verse 5, *"apart from me, you can do **nothing**."*

Perhaps those are hard words for you to swallow. You may be thinking, "But I do things apart from Christ all the time." Dear friend, Jesus is referring to your ability to produce fruit. You are incapable of growing fruit without Jesus. And one particular quality distinguishes Jesus' fruit from all else in this world: it will *last* (John 15:16).

Sure, you can make bricks all day long, planning and maneuvering to accomplish your plans. You can stack those bricks and pile them high, earning the praise of onlookers while perhaps even hoping to draw the gaze of the Father. Your efforts, however, will prove fruitless, and the monument you build with sweat and tears will end up a pile of rubble.

We must remember that we serve as *dependents* of the one true God; we are not God, Himself. Consider **1 Corinthians 3:5-9.**

> *We are incapable of growing fruit without Jesus.*

- According to **verse 5**, how do servants of Jesus come up with their tasks?

_____

- What do **verses 6-7** teach about our ability to *grow* things?

_____

- How will each servant be rewarded (**verse 8**)?

_____

- What is the "one purpose" mentioned in this verse?

_____

"For we are God's fellow workers; you are God's field, God's building" (verse 9). God alone holds the ability to grow fruit for His kingdom, but He sent us His Son to lead us and equip us to participate in His work. As we draw near to the Word to hear His instruction and obediently follow Jesus to complete the

individual tasks assigned to us, God brings forth the harvest. Dear one, your individual blessing in Christ is tied to God's collective plan for His kingdom.

Let's consider what happens when we refuse to cooperate. Please read **Isaiah 5:1-6**, picturing Jesus as the beloved owner of the vineyard. Ask God to speak to your heart about the condition of His church.

- According to **verse 1**, what was the condition of the hill on which He planted His vineyard?

_____

- What did He do in preparation for His crop (**verse 2**)?

_____

_____

_____

- What happened when He surveyed the crop?

_____

Your individual blessing in Christ is tied to God's collective plan for His kingdom.

Hear the sadness in His heart as He asks the question in verse 4, *"What more could have been done for my vineyard than I have done for it?"*

Indeed, what more could Jesus have done? He gave up His own life that we might be released from the power of sin and death, making us bearers of the fruit of life ourselves! Yet gazing at His crop, He didn't recognize the fruit that should have emerged from what He planted.

In Jeremiah 2:21-22 God declares, *"I had planted you like a choice vine of sound and reliable stock. How then did you turn against me into a corrupt, wild vine? Although you wash yourself with soda and use an abundance of soap, the stain of your guilt is still before me."*

God sees the difference between the counterfeit and the true. Our brick-making and washing of ourselves does not deceive Him. He will not be mocked, and, sadly, we will always reap what we sow (Galatians 6:7).

- According to **Isaiah 5:5-6**, what did the owner of the vineyard do in response to what He saw?

_____

_____

_____

- Based on what we've already studied, what do briers and thorns appearing within the vineyard signify (see page 55)?

_____

(see page 55)

> *"Arise, shine, for your light has come, and the glory of the LORD rises upon you."*
> —ISAIAH 60:1

As the Gardener has surveyed His vineyard over the centuries, I imagine His emotions have risen and fallen with the changing landscape of His harvest field. To His great joy, the early church brought forth an abundant harvest. But as time passed and zeal for the glory of the Lord diminished, the appearance of its branches and their fruit began to change.

Praise God that throughout history, no matter how far His people strayed, turning their backs on His will and going their own way, He has always preserved for Himself a faithful and believing remnant (Isaiah 37:31). And in moments when all seems lost and His people are hardly recognizable as His, He raises His remnant to stir His people to return to Him again with wholehearted devotion.

Our time has come, dear one. The moment has arrived for Christ's church to arise and once again become what God designed it to be. He has done His part. He chose a fertile hillside and planted the choicest Vine (John 15:1). Then He set about watering the Vine He had planted in the earth with Living Water, poured out by the release of His Spirit (John 7:38-39). Now He surveys what He has planted and looks for a crop of good fruit.

Beloved, what does He see when His eyes rest on you?

day 3: FILTHY RAGS BECOME CLEAN LINEN

In day 2 of our second week together, we discovered that God's purpose in saving us exceeds merely demonstrating His love for us. He desires to reveal Himself through His chosen people. We witness God's power and glory as He produces fruit in His children, grown through the one true Vine.

- According to **Matthew 3:8**, what type of fruit is God looking for as He surveys His vineyard?

_____

Repentance is the heart motivation that compels us to put our faith in Jesus. As the Holy Spirit reveals our wayward path and convicts us of our guilt, we abandon our former lives and determine to let Jesus lead us instead of continuing to go our own way. Fruit *"in keeping with repentance"* would be fruit that flows from obedience to Him.

Please read **1 Peter 1:1-2**, asking God for understanding of His Word.

- According to **verse 2**, how are we chosen?

_____

- What two things are we chosen for?

  1. _____

  2. _____

- These two things are accomplished *through* what?

_____

Scripture teaches that members of Christ's kingdom are chosen according to the foreknowledge of God. What does God know in advance that moves Him to choose us? He knows who will humble themselves in a posture of obedience to His will and who will seek to exalt their own. Remember Saul and David? God sees straight into the hearts of men. Try as we might, we cannot deceive Him.

Today's Truth:

WE KNOW THAT WE HAVE COME TO KNOW HIM IF WE KEEP HIS COMMANDS. THE MAN WHO SAYS, "I KNOW HIM," BUT DOES NOT DO WHAT HE COMMANDS IS A LIAR, AND THE TRUTH IS NOT IN HIM.
—1 JOHN 2:3-4

Verse two also teaches that we have been selected by God for two things: the cleansing of our sin through the sprinkling of Christ's blood and obedience to Jesus. Dear one, the Gospel of Jesus Christ proclaims a message of obedience.

- According to **2 Thessalonians 1:8**, who will be punished with everlasting destruction when Jesus is revealed in blazing fire?

_____

_____

So, did Christ preach a Gospel of faith or obedience?

Confusion stems from the fact that we've tried to separate the two. In reality, they are two sides of the same coin. To live by faith is to actively trust. Remember, Jesus calls us to follow Him. Our obedience becomes our expression of faith as we follow where He leads.

To live by faith means to actively trust through obedience.

• We express faith as we obediently follow where Jesus leads.

I hope you have already come to recognize Scripture's truth that our good works, in and of themselves, hold no value in the eyes of God. We can "do" and build and plan, but unless our actions are filtered through obedience to God's particular will for us expressed through Christ, our works are meaningless. In fact, it might surprise you to see how God describes them in Scripture.

- According to **Isaiah 64:6**, to what does God compare our righteous acts?

_____

I know this might be difficult to wrap your mind around, but all of the "good works" you do apart from Jesus appear as filthy rags in the sight of our Holy God. Why? Because sin, that which makes us unclean, is defined by disregard for God's will. He's looking for sheep who will humbly follow the voice of the Shepherd (John 10:4). Sheep who stray from Him, even if they're being kind to the other sheep, are still guilty of rebellion. Rebellion against His will is sin, *"and like the wind our sins sweep us away."*

Praise God that faith in Jesus Christ removes the stain of our guilt through the sprinkling of His blood and allows us to take on His righteousness, forever freeing us from sin's penalty. But our continual obedience to Christ's leadership remains pivotal to maintaining our blameless standing before God. He calls us to follow. Ignoring His direction to produce our own works is sin. Without His prompting and empowerment calling us to action, the things we do—even the seemingly righteous, compassionate, loving things we do for Him—remain "unclean" because they spring from wrong motives. He alone is King, and Lord of our steps. God credits faith—active trust—as righteousness.

Please read **Romans 4:3-8**, asking God for understanding of His Word.

- According to **verse 3**, why did God credit Abraham with righteousness?

_____

- To whom will God credit righteousness (**verse 5**)?

_____

- What blessing is given to those God credits with righteousness apart from works (**verses 7-8**)?

_____

_____

Sometimes "good things" we do can remain unclean because they spring from wrong motives.

• Jesus desires to be the source of our choices and decisions.

As we consider the subject of faith and works, let's reflect on James 2:17: *"faith by itself, if it is not accompanied by action, is dead."* Ask God to deepen your understanding of the relationship between the two, and please read **James 2:14- 24.**

- What does James suggest by his questions in **verse 14**?

_____

- What did James reveal about the relationship between his faith and deeds in **verse 18**?

_____

• What does **verse 19** suggest?

_____

_____

• We saw earlier in Romans 4:3 that Abraham was credited with righteousness by God because he *believed* Him. Why does **verse 21** say he was considered righteous?

_____

• **Verse 22** explains the inconsistency. Fill in the following blanks.

"*You see that his _____and his _____ were _____, and his _____ was _____ _____by what he_____.*"

Dear one, according to Scripture, without action to complete our faith, we have not yet *believed*. Until we have believed God, trusting Him through action, He will not credit us with righteousness. That's why confessing Jesus' lordship over our lives remains pivotal to our salvation; committing our lives to follow Him as Lord is the action that completes our faith and seals us as His own. And once we are His, our choice to persist in actively trusting Him through obedience to His commands allows Him to manifest His righteousness in our lives, and "*sanctify us through and through*" (1 Thessalonians 5:23).

Jesus isn't keeping track of your good works, beloved. He's keeping track of how often you trust Him!

God told Abraham that He would give him a son through whom He would bless all peoples of the earth. Then He asked Abraham to trust Him with the life of that very son. Abraham believed God and did as he was told, trusting God to keep His word and fulfill His promise to him. His faith, demonstrated through his actions, ushered him into God's blessing and allowed God to credit Abraham with the righteousness that comes from faith.

And the scripture was fulfilled that says, "Abraham believed God, and it was credited to him as righteousness," and he was called God's friend (JAMES 2:23).

God longs to bless you as well. As you draw near to Jesus and He communicates God's plans for you to your heart, you have a decision to make. You must choose whether or not you will trust Him and obediently follow His instructions by faith. Your obedience allows Him to credit your works as righteous.

As we close today, join me in glimpsing one of your blessings to come. Please read **Revelation 19:6-8.**

• According to **verse 7**, what event does this passage describe?

_____

• What has happened to bring about this wedding?

_____

• What will the bride of Christ wear on her wedding day (**verse 8**)?

_____

• What does fine linen represent?

_____

*"Fine linen stands for the **righteous** acts of the saints."* Do you see it, dear one? Faith transforms our filthy rags into clean, white, fine linen. For our works to hold eternal value, Jesus must be their source. As we faithfully and obediently trust Him to govern our steps, the quality of our work changes. Every act prompted by Christ and completed by our faithful obedience to His command, transforms from a filthy rag into a garment of beautiful cloth. At Christ's return, you will wear the splendor of the fruit of your faith.

*With this in mind, we constantly pray for you, that our God may count you worthy of his calling, and that by his power he may fulfill every **good purpose of yours** and every **act prompted by your faith***
(2 THESSALONIANS 1:11, EMPHASIS MINE).

day 4: PRESENT YOUR FREEWILL OFFERING

Psalm 127:1 presents this unwavering truth:

*"Unless the LORD builds the house,
its builders labor in vain."*

God meticulously and purposefully works in our midst, building His dwelling place stone by stone. He has chosen to offer us the privilege of participating in His work. After all, love and relationship motivate Him. Those who answer His call, humbly yielding to His will and allowing God to shape them into the living stones with which He builds, enjoy the blessing of participating in the divine.

We will also inherit the house at its completion. Oh, glorious day!

God's nature remains unchanging, and so do His desires for His people. As we examine our role in the building of God's house, we are wise to remember His expectations of those who have gone before.

Today we will journey back to the desert with Moses and the Israelites to consider God's instructions for the construction of His first earthly dwelling after the fall, the tabernacle. Please read **Exodus 25:1-9**.

- How did they determine which offerings would be brought to the Lord for the building of the tabernacle (**verse 2**)?

_____

- According to **verse 8**, what was the purpose of the sanctuary they would build?

_____

- According to what pattern would the people build it (**verse 9**)?

_____

I hope by now you readily recognize a familiar theme. God instructed the people to build His dwelling according to His specific plan and pattern. He held the master blueprint. He didn't allow them to improvise. Their job was simply to follow His lead and contribute to the work. How would they contribute? Each man would give as his heart prompted him.

Exodus 35:20-29 reveals the overwhelming response from the people.

- How does **verse 21** describe the people who participated in bringing offerings?

_____

*All the Israelite men and women who were **willing** brought to the LORD **freewill offerings** for all the work the LORD through Moses had commanded them to do* (VERSE 29, EMPHASIS MINE).

Two important truths present themselves in this passage.

1. God will build His dwelling only with *freewill* offerings.
2. God will accomplish His ultimate purpose through community.

Let's take a few moments to consider the first truth. Verse 21 describes the willing vessels God used to build His first earthly house as those *"whose heart moved him."* A common thread appears in the circumstances surrounding the rebuilding of His second earthly dwelling, the temple in Jerusalem.

- Read **Ezra 1:1-2**. According to **verse 1**, what motivated Cyrus to make this proclamation?

_____

- What did God appoint Cyrus to do (**verse 2**)?

_____

Cyrus, King of Persia, was a pagan king with no ties to the God of Israel. And yet he was the man through whom God would bring about the restoration of His people and the rebuilding of His temple after their fall into exile. How? The Lord moved Cyrus' heart to respond to His desires.

Cyrus wasn't the only one who responded to God with obedience.

• According to **verse 5**, who responded to Cyrus' proclamation?

_____

Your gift of obedience is your freewill offering.

Each time God erected His dwelling place, He built the structure through men and women obedient to His prompting of their hearts. People brought forth freewill offerings in response to the invitation of God's Spirit, and together they built a sanctuary for the Lord, a place for Him to dwell among men.

Now the dwelling of God is *within* men (Ephesians 2:21-22)!

• What does **1 Corinthians 6:19-20** teach about the current temple of God?

_____

_____

In salvation, we presented ourselves to Jesus as a freewill offering. Our offerings continue as we respond to the movement of His Spirit within our hearts. Our gift of obedience will result in a spectacular sight!

One of Jesus' last recorded acts in Scripture before His arrest and execution is a prayer He uttered to the Father on behalf of those He was leaving behind. As you read **John 17:20-23**, contemplate the reality that His last thoughts were of you.

• What specifically did He pray for us in **verse 21**?

_____

• What is His purpose in making us one?

_____

- Why did Jesus give us His glory (**verse 22**)?

_____

- According to **verse 23**, how will the world recognize that God sent us Jesus?

_____

   - Our *complete unity* will also show them what?

_____

We will only truly express God's love when we are one in Him and one with each other. Consider the face of the alternative. Please read **1 Corinthians 3:1-4**, asking God to speak truth to the depths of your heart.

Quarreling within the body of Christ indicates spiritual immaturity.

- Why couldn't Paul address these brothers as "spiritual" (**verse 1**)?

_____

- How did he define "worldly" in **verse 3**?

_____

I love his claim that they were acting like "mere men." Do you recall our study of Stephen in week three? Those housing the indwelling presence of the Holy Spirit are no longer limited to the natural. In Christ, the natural should be overcome and empowered by the divine.

Remember that the grace poured out to us through Jesus offers us the opportunity to live as light in a dark world. Jealousy and quarreling have no place within the body of Christ. Their presence indicates a quenching of the Spirit and the rise of our flesh within us.

- According to **James 4:1**, what causes fights and quarrels among people?

_____

Verse 2 adds, "*You want something but don't get it.*" Our natural state revolves around this principal condition: "I want what I want when I want it." Our own desires keep us quarreling with one another and block the flow of Christ's love in and through us.

Jesus asked the Father for *one thing* for His church as He prepared to leave this earth. He asked that **all** who would believe on His name would become *one* in Him.

Allow your mind to settle on that thought. Jesus prayed that thousands upon thousands of those who would believe on His name would become one unified expression of the glory that flows from who He is. That glory would be **witnessed** by the world as an expression of God's love.

So often we allow our personal preferences to dictate our convictions. The bonds that we feel toward our race, our denomination, our traditions, even our gender, move us to take sides and oppose one another.

Consider this truth: Jesus **always** prays according to the Father's will.

Unity in the body of Christ can only take place as we willingly lay down our personal desires and let Jesus replace them with His.

- According to **1 John 5:14-15**, what confidence do we have in approaching God in prayer?

_____

_____

Jesus' prayer to His Father has already been answered. One day ALL who truly believe on Him will arise in one accord. The boundary walls that man has made will hold no power to separate this growing union of hearts. Jesus will take His rightful place as Head, abolishing the false authority of the pride of man. The walls of division will crumble as He leads His members in beautiful harmony, and God's love and Christ's glory in Him will be evident to all.

Lord, hasten the day!

day 5: GOLD, SILVER, AND COSTLY STONES

We've spent the last four weeks looking at God's plans to build His kingdom and have sought His help to determine our role in the building process. I pray you've encountered a new revelation of Jesus and have gained some insight into who you really are as well. We will conclude our time together with a look at the judgment to come for those in Christ. Please read **1 Corinthians 3:10-15**.

- What warning does Paul give in **verse 10**?

_____

- **Verse 11** reminds us that the foundation for all things has been laid. What (or who) is that foundation?

_____

We began our study in week one establishing the certain truth that Jesus is our Cornerstone, the one sure foundation on which we must build. Matthew 7:24 taught us that in order to build on that foundation, we must draw near to hear Jesus' words to us, and then trust Him by doing what He says. Today, 1 Corinthians 3:10 cautions us again to be careful how we build.

- **Verse 12** lists six building materials. Based on their similarities, separate them into two categories, each consisting of three items.

    1. _____

    2. _____

- According to **verse 13**, how will the quality of our work be revealed when Christ returns?

_____

- What will happen if your work survives the fire (**verse 14**)?

_____

Today's Truth:

IF ANY MAN BUILDS ON THIS FOUNDATION USING GOLD, SILVER, COSTLY STONES, WOOD, HAY OR STRAW, HIS WORK WILL BE SHOWN FOR WHAT IT IS, BECAUSE THE DAY WILL BRING IT TO LIGHT. IT WILL BE REVEALED WITH FIRE, AND THE FIRE WILL TEST THE QUALITY OF EACH MAN'S WORK.
—1 CORINTHIANS 3:12-13

- What will happen to you if what you have built burns in the flames (**verse 15**)?

_____

He will suffer loss. We don't often think of Christ's return holding moments of sadness for God's own. The Day of Judgment is heralded as a time of great rejoicing for those in His kingdom. And it surely will be! But for some in Christ, the all-surpassing joy of coming face to face with their Redeemer will be pierced by the ache of loss as all that has remained hidden becomes disclosed.

- What will the Lord do when He comes, according to **1 Corinthians 4:5**?

_____

_____

When the fires of judgment come, light will penetrate all darkness and reveal the hidden motives of men's hearts. For those who have put their faith in Jesus, offering their lives to Him as Lord, salvation is guaranteed (verse 15); we needn't fear the judgment of the condemned. We will, however, give an accounting before God as the fire tests the quality of the life we lived under the banner of Jesus' name.

When we ask Jesus to save us and confess Him as Lord of our lives, we enter a covenant with God, a binding covenant, sealed in Christ's blood. With our confession of faith, we promise God that we will cease living according to our own will and resolve to live the remainder of our days exalting Jesus as the Lord of glory. God provides the means for us to keep our agreement. He will then measure our eternal blessing by how faithfully we kept our word.

As the fire consumes all that is temporal, those who have strayed from the foundation on which they committed to build their lives will see what should have been. Perhaps this is one reason we're told God *"will wipe every tear from their eyes"* (Revelation 21:4) when He ushers in the new heaven and the new earth. I pray yours will be tears of rejoicing when perfection finally comes, and that you will leave a legacy that survives the flames.

To ensure God's blessing, 1 Corinthians 3 teaches that we must build with gold, silver, and costly stones. Let's consider what each of these elements represent in Scripture.

GOLD

Please read **1 Peter 1:3-9**, asking God's Spirit to interpret His Word.

• What great gift has God given us in Jesus (**verse 3**)?

_____

• How does Scripture describe our inheritance in Him (**verse 4**)?

_____

• What gives us access to the shield of God's power (**verse 5**)?

_____

• How long does the suffering of grief in trials last (**verse 6**)?

_____

• What two results potentially come from our trials, according to **verse 7**?

    1. _____

    2. _____

Note that Scripture describes our faith as *"of greater worth than gold."* Our fiery trials will reveal two things: whether our faith is genuine, and whether our faith will result in praise, glory, and honor at Jesus' return.

Consider the characteristics of gold; its *purity* measures its *value*. Gold also symbolizes authority; gold is the gift of kings.

Centuries ago, Magi traveled from the east in search of a newborn king.

Gold: works done in obedience to Jesus, completed faith

• We build with gold as we obediently follow where Jesus leads and live out God's plan instead of our own.

- According to **Matthew 2:11**, what was the first thing they did upon finding Jesus in Bethlehem?

_____

- What was the first gift they presented to Him in recognition of His status as King?

_____

Our works of gold, dear one, are those built in recognition of Jesus as the King of Kings. They are our acts of worship, stemming from a heart bowed down in submission to His will. We build with gold as we obediently follow where He leads. As we trust Him in obedience, persevering for Him even when we don't understand, our faith is proved genuine and comes forth as gold.

Silver: sanctification, cooperating with Jesus to rid us of sin • We build with silver as we allow Jesus to purify our hearts and transform us into His image.

SILVER

Scripture associates silver with refiner's fire. *"For you, O God, tested us; you refined us like silver"* (Psalm 66:10).

- According to **Isaiah 48:10**, how does God refine us?

_____

Silver emerges as we allow our fiery trials to sanctify us. Read **Proverbs 25:4-5**.

- What happens when silver is heated (**verse 4**)?

_____

- To what does God compare this process in **verse 5**?

_____

Jesus died to remove sin and its consequence from our lives. As we cooperate with His cleansing work, allowing Him to purify our hearts and rid us of our bondage to sin, we build with silver. Please read **2 Corinthians 4:16-18**.

- In Christ, what is happening to us day by day (**verse 16**)?

_____

- What do our troubles achieve for us (**verse 17**)?

_____

Have you considered the reality that out of His great love for you, God purposes trials for your life so you may live out your greatest blessing in Him? Our trials don't merely affect this temporal life. What we allow God to do in us through them will mark our eternity!

This life is a mere breath, a shadow of the glory to come when Christ's final enemies are defeated and He reigns forever in perfection and righteousness. Eternity, dear one, is where you spend forever. Perhaps that perspective can help us to better understand the illogical statement found in James 1:2-4.

> _Consider it_ **pure joy**_, my brothers, whenever you face trials of many kinds, because you know that the testing of your faith develops perseverance. Perseverance must finish its work so that you may be mature and complete,_ **not lacking in anything** _(emphasis mine)._

Your God desires that you lack nothing of the blessing available to you in Jesus. So, He has ordained for you _"light and momentary troubles"_ to achieve for you _"an eternal glory that far outweighs them all"_ (2 Corinthians 4:17).

Will you allow Jesus to skim off your impurities and generate pure silver in you? We can let our trials and troubles overcome us, ignoring God's purpose in them. Or, we can _"fix our eyes not on what is seen, but on what is unseen. For what is seen is temporary, but what is unseen is eternal"_ (2 Corinthians 4:18).

COSTLY STONES

Revelation 21:2 describes God's Holy City, _"the new Jerusalem, coming down out of heaven from God, prepared as a bride beautifully dressed for her husband."_ The chapter goes on to describe the city in great detail.

- According to **Revelation 21:19**, what are the foundations of the city walls decorated with?

_____

- What does **Ephesians 2:21-22** teach that God's building is made up of?

_____

Costly Stones: souls won for Christ's kingdom • We build with costly stones as we impact lives for Christ and lead others to discover and know Him.

Perhaps the "costly stones" we offer to the Lord at His return are the people we reached for His kingdom. As we become light and life, sharing the hope we have in Jesus and leading others to find Him, these precious, new followers also become living stones, taking on the sparkling brilliance of Christ's light as they faithfully follow Him. Our willingness to fulfill His Great Commission will display itself as the precious stones adorning the foundation walls of our eternal city. Each will be uniquely and gloriously cut, and their colors will express wondrous variety.

> *I looked and there before me was a great multitude that no one could count, from every nation, tribe, people and language, standing before the throne and in front of the Lamb. They were wearing white robes and were holding palm branches in their hands (REVELATION 7:9).*

What will your offering consist of, dear one? What monument do you build with the life you live? Do you allow Jesus to bring forth gold, silver, and precious stones, or do you build using flammable wood, hay, and straw? You either construct "of a palace on the one hand, of a mud hut on the other" (Lightfoot).[3] At the end of days, only the palace will remain.

Build the palace, beloved. The glory of the palace of the Most

_____

3 Robertson, A. (1997). *Word Pictures in the New Testament* (1 Co 3:12). Oak Harbor: Logos Research Systems.

High will never fade, and He will warmly welcome you within its walls. Suffering and disease will cease, and you will live forever blanketed in the warmth of perfect joy, peace, and love, cast by the light of the Son Himself.

> *"Behold, I am coming soon! My reward is with me, and I will give to everyone according to what he has done. I am the Alpha and Omega, the First and the Last, the Beginning and the End.*
> *Blessed are those who wash their robes, that they may have the right to the tree of life, and may go through the gates into the city."*
> REVELATION 22:12-14

Reflections on Week 4

"My food," said Jesus, *"is to do the will of Him who sent me and to finish His work."*

JOHN 4:34

Open in prayer and invite the Spirit to provide understanding during your discussion.

Day one:
1. Have you ever felt like you were missing something in your Christian walk, or that your experience didn't measure up to God's promises? If so, why do you think that is?

2. What do you think it means to put your faith in Jesus?

3. **Matthew 7:21** teaches that not everyone who calls Jesus "Lord" will enter heaven. Does it surprise you that Jesus will turn people away at His return, even people who appeared to serve Him?
   • These people trusted that the works they did in Jesus' name would save them. What were Jesus' reasons for turning them away (**verses 21, 23**)?
   • How can you know for certain that you belong to Him?

Day two:
1. What do you think it means that Christ is the "head" of the church (**Colossians 1:18**)? Discuss the analogy between Christ's church and the workings of our physical bodies from page 14.
   • How can you apply this concept in your life? In your church?

2. **2 Corinthians 11:14** warns us that our enemy masquerades as an angel of light (p.15). What danger does that present for us and how can we avoid it?

3. According to Scripture, every believer possesses the ability to hear God (**John 8:47**).
   • Do you hear Him? If you don't, what do you think might be keeping you from that blessing?

Day three:
1. How does your relationship with Jesus differ from what He describes in **John 10** (p.18)?

2. In **John 5:39-40**, Jesus warns that we can diligently study His Word and yet miss its life (p.20). How do you think that's possible?
   - Do you tend to approach Scripture like a textbook or an opportunity to meet with God?

3. What do you think it means to be a "true worshipper" (**John 4:23-24**)? (p.21)
   - Discuss ways that we can interact with the Spirit as we read God's Word.

4. Share a time God spoke through His Word to guide you along His plan for you.

Day four:
1. Do you ever struggle with wanting to do one thing, but actually doing something else?
   - Why do you think we often fail to follow through on our good intentions?

2. **Galatians 5:16-18** teaches that each one of us battles between following our old sinful nature and the Holy Spirit we receive at salvation (p.25). The result of allowing that conflict to continue will always end in sin (**verse 17**). Why do you think that is?
   - What do we need to do to end that battle and resolve the conflict?
   - Do these verses help you to better understand your own personal struggles?

Day five:
1. **Proverbs 14:12** teaches that what seems right to us often leads to death (p.28).
   - Discuss the dangers of acting on our feelings.

2. What can you do to present yourself to God as a living sacrifice (p.29)?
   - How can being willing to embrace God's will place you in a position to discern it?

3. Based on Jesus' words in **Luke 9:23**, what do you think it really means to follow Him (p.31)?

4. Share testimony of how the death or end of something opened the doorway to a new blessing.

Close in prayer, inviting Jesus to change your hearts with the truths you're learning. Encourage group members to spend dedicated time with Jesus and complete their daily lessons.

Open in prayer and invite the Spirit to guide your discussion. Encourage group members to share how God spoke to them through the homework.

Day one:

1. In **John 14:21**, Jesus promises to show Himself to those who love Him. What do you think that means?
   • Share testimony of ways He has revealed Himself in your life.

2. Jesus said the most important command in all of Scripture is to love God with all that we are (**Mark 12:29-30**). How does God define love, according to **1 John 5:3** (p.37)?

3. Discuss how the characteristics of agape love differ from earthly love (p.37).
   • What do we need to do to love with agape?

Day two:

1. **2 Thessalonians 1:10** reveals that Jesus will be glorified in His people when He returns. How does Jesus being gloried "in" us differ from being glorified "by" us?

2. Everything God does finds its root in one purpose: seeing His will lived out on earth. According to **Ephesians 2:10**, for what purpose are we saved (p.41)?
   • How does this relate to God's expectations of you once you are His?

3. Before God ever sent Jesus, He shared His purpose in establishing the new covenant in **Ezekiel 36:21-23**: to reveal His holiness through His people. What does that mean for you?
   • Do you recognize His Spirit moving you to follow Him?

Day three:

1. Can you relate to the opening story?
   • How can you apply the principle in your own life?

2. God replaced Saul as King over Israel because he failed to follow His instructions. What reasoning did Saul offer for his disobedience (p.48)?

- Do you find you also tend to justify your own partial obedience to God? What are your reasons?

3. How do we sometimes offer "sacrifices" to the Lord rather than obedience?

Day four:
1. Israel's elders asked for a king because they wanted to be like everyone else. How were the people rejecting God by requesting a king (p.51)?
    - Do you believe you are rejecting God when you insist on your own will?

2. God warned the people that insisting on having their own way would cost them. How did they respond in **1 Samuel 8:19** (p.52)?
    - How do we often make that same choice the Israelites made?

3. **Galatians 6:7-8** declares that every one of us will reap what we sow through our choices (p.53). What does it mean to "sow to please the Spirit" instead of sowing to please your sin nature?

Day five:
1. What happened when David tried to honor God by bringing the Ark of the Covenant to Jerusalem (**2 Samuel 6:1-11**)? (p.56)
    - How would you have responded to God in those circumstances?
    - Why didn't God bless David's efforts (p.57)?
2. According to **Deuteronomy 10:13**, why does God give us decrees or instructions (p.58)?
    - Based on David's experience, is ignorance an excuse when we disregard God's instruction?
    - How can we ensure that the things we do for God will receive His favor and blessing?

Allow a time of sharing personal needs and prayer requests. Encourage group members to persevere in completing their lessons. Expect to see God reveal Himself!

week 3 DISCUSSION GUIDE

Open in prayer and encourage group members to share how God spoke to them through the homework.

Day one:

1. **John 11:40** states that those who believe will see God's glory (p.62). How have you seen God's glory revealed in your life?

2. According to **Exodus 33:16**, what distinguishes God's own from the rest of the world (p.63)?
   - Discuss the difference between God's omnipresence [ability to be present everywhere at all times] and His Manifest Presence (p.63).
   - Considering Moses' experience with God (p.64), do you think people should be able to tell we've been in God's presence?

3. According to **2 Corinthians 3:18,** what should be happening to each of us who belong to Jesus (p.65)?

Day two:

1. In **John 20:22**, Jesus breathed on His disciples and said, "Receive the Holy Spirit." What do you think happened in that moment?

2. What does it mean to you that you have been "sealed" [secured, owned] by the Holy Spirit?

3. How do you think being "sealed" by the Spirit differs from being "filled" by Him?
   - Discuss: You will only be filled to the extent that you are yielded.

Day three:

1. According to **Ephesians 3:19**, God desires to fill us with the full measure of Himself (p.72)! What does that mean to you?

2. What does the disciples' experience in **Acts 4:29-31** teach about what is available to us as believers (p.74)?

3. Share your thoughts on Stephen's story from pages 75-76.
   - What enabled Stephen to stand firm in the face of hatred?
   - What do you need to do to become extraordinary like Stephen?

Day four:

1. Do you believe God's promise in **2 Peter 1:3-4** that you have been given all that you need to successfully live a godly life (p.77)?

2. Based on **Psalm19:13**, what do you understand blameless to mean (p.78)?
   - What distinguishes willful sin from other transgressions? Can you sin "unintentionally"?

3. Has it ever occurred to you that God doesn't hear all your prayers (**Isaiah 59:2**) (p.80)?
   - What can you do to ensure your prayers are heard (**2 Chronicles 7:14**)?

Day five:

1. Discuss the 3 stages of sanctification from page 82.

2. Based on **Matthew 5:17-20**, how does grace call us to a higher standard of righteousness than the law did (p.84)?
   - Does this differ from your understanding of grace?

3. According to **John 8:32**, we must know the truth before it can set us free from sin's chains (p.86).
   - Discuss these three truths we must know before we can be released from any bondage:
     - Know the One who is Truth – (**John 17:3, John 14:6**)
     - Know the Truth of God's Word – (**John 17:17**)
     - Know the truth about yourself – (**Psalm 139:23-24**)

Close your time together by asking God to help you live blamelessly. Commit to surrender wholeheartedly to the leadership of His Spirit and allow His grace to release you from sin's chains. Invite Him to fill you with His presence so that you may live through His power!

Open in prayer and encourage group members to share how God spoke to them through the homework.

Day one:

1. How did the building of the tower of Babel demonstrate rebellion against God?

2. Why do you think we find rest when we let Jesus lead (**Matthew 11:29**) (p.92)?

3. Discuss the differences between a "brick maker" and a "living stone."
   • Why do you think our "bricks" are unacceptable to God (**1 Peter 2:5**)?
   • Share your own stories of how you've worn yourself out trying to make bricks.

Day two:

1. Considering that God is at work, building a kingdom according to His perfect plan, why do you think **Psalm 46:10** is so important to put into practice?
   • How does building with our own works exalt us instead of God?

2. What rises up in you when you read Jesus' words, "apart from me you can do nothing?" Do you believe Him?
   • How does making bricks differ from producing fruit (p.96)?

3. What does **Isaiah 5:1-6** speak to you about how God sees His church (p. 97)?

Day three:

1. According to **1 Peter 1:2**, we have been chosen for obedience to Jesus Christ.
   • How do you understand the role of obedience in the life of faith (p.99)?

2. God describes our "righteous acts" as filthy rags in **Isaiah 64:6**. What do you think makes them unclean (p.100)?

3. According to **James 2:22**, what makes our faith incomplete (p.102)?
   • Based on **verse 23**, have we "believed" if we haven't acted on our faith?
   • Discuss how you can be certain you are truly living by godly faith that pleases God.

Day four:

1. Why do you think God only uses *freewill* offerings to build His dwelling place (p.105)?

2. Jesus knelt to pray for the unity of believers before He went to the cross (p.106). One day every follower of Christ will be one with Him and one with each other (**John 17:21**). What will it take for us to truly become the One Body, without conflict or dissention?
   - What will our unity reveal (p.107)?

3. Based on **1 Corinthians 3:1-4**, what does a lack of unity demonstrate?
   - How does Scripture define "worldliness"?

Day five:

1. Read **1 Corinthians 3:10-13** together. When Christ returns, the fires of judgment will test the quality of our work (p.109).
   - What will happen to believers who ceased building on the foundation of Jesus Christ?
   - Discuss how the choices we make each day will affect our eternal reward.

2. What does gold represent in Scripture?
   - How do we build with gold?

3. Scripture associates silver with what?
   - How do we build with silver?

4. What do costly stones represent?
   - Are you building with gold, silver, and precious stones?

Close your time together by praying that the seeds planted in your hearts from God's Word will be faithfully watered and grown by the Holy Spirit. Join together in praying the prayer of commitment on the next page, asking God to stir your heart to desire what you pray. Commit to live each day as living stones, following Jesus to fulfill His plans for your lives.

prayer of commitment

Lord Jesus, I exalt You as the Lord of Glory. I acknowledge that all things were made through You and for You. You are my King, and I desire to build my life solely on the foundation of Your will for me.

Help me draw nearer to You. Fill me with a desire to remain in Your presence. Awaken me each day with a longing to meet with You in Your Word. Open my ears to hear You speak to me. Teach me to recognize Your voice. When I hear from You, give me the courage to trust You and follow.

Cleanse me by the power of Your Spirit. Rid me of my divided heart, so that I may be filled by You. Expose the darkness within me. Allow me to see what You see. As You shine Your light on my sin, give me the strength to reject it. Empower me to live for You alone, blameless in my generation. Help me believe that through You I can conquer my sin and be free!

Use me, Lord, to love the world. Cause me to think with Your thoughts, to speak with Your words, and to love with Your love. Help me to stop making bricks out of my own strength. Shape me into a living stone, moved and empowered by Your Spirit. Make me a vessel of Your glory!

Lord Jesus, make me ready for Your return. Bring forth gold, silver, and precious stones from my life, that I may present a bountiful offering to You when You come again. Thank You for all that You have done for me, and for all You are going to do through me.

In the Name above every name, Jesus—my King and my Glory,

Amen

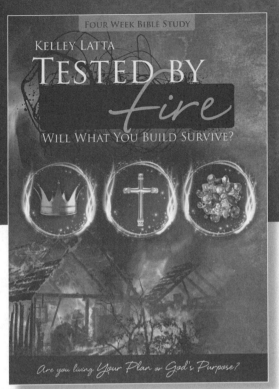

Enhance your journey through *Tested by Fire* with these Free Resources!

For Your Small Group or Bible Study:

- Optional discussion guide for your introductory session to help prepare your group and define the goals of the study.

- Printable weekly discussion guides to help direct conversation.

- Video teaching sessions by Kelley that give additional insight into the lessons.

Not a Part of a Bible Study?

- Register for online Bible study to have videos and book assignments emailed directly to you each week.

- Participate in online discussion through our website.

Visit KelleyLattaMinistries.com

Kelley
LATTA
MINISTRIES, LLC